TREADMILL TRAINING FOR RUNNERS

RICK MORRIS

SHAMROCK COVE

Treadmill Training for Runners

Published by:
Shamrock Cove Publishing, Inc.
Post Office Box 631100
Littleton, Colorado 80163-1100

Copyright © 2009 by Rick Morris
First Printing 2009

Printed in the United States of America

10 9 8 7 6 5 4 3 2 1

ISBN 13: 978-1-931088-03-9

Library of Congress Control Number: 2004091679

Notice to Readers:
This book is intended as a reference only and is not intended as a replacement for professional fitness and medical advice. You should get clearance from your physician before engaging in any form of exercise.

Contents

1

Confessions of a Treadmill Junkie

In the not too distant past, the term treadmill brought up all sorts of negative images. The definition of "treadmill" is - "A habitual, laborious, often tiresome course of action." That's enough to give a runner a textbook case of the "willies!." The only runners seen on treadmills in those days were hooked up to hoses, plugs and wires to provide researchers with information on respiration, VO_2 max and stresses on joints and muscles. That image will scare away even the toughest runners!

Treadmills of the past did their part to earn their reputation as an instrument of torture. They were big, clunky, ugly and loud enough to drown out a jet engine at full throttle. They were hard to look at and even harder to run on. The belts didn't operate smoothly and the whole machine rocked and rolled like the deck of a sailboat in a squall.

On top of all this, treadmills were stigmatized. Runners simply didn't believe that running on a treadmill was "real" running. They also thought that anyone caught running on one was not a "real" runner. Even if you wanted to run on the treadmill you wouldn't risk the humiliation of being seen on it.

In those days, runners didn't trust the training benefits of treadmill training. They felt that the treadmill wouldn't give them the same physiological improvements that free range running did.

Well - things have changed. Beginning in the early 1990's, the treadmill boom began. In 1987, 4.4 million  Americans owned and exercised on treadmills. Ten years later, in 1997, 36.1 million owned treadmills -a whopping 772% increase. Those numbers are still increasing today. One would assume that an increase of that magnitude would be due to an rise in the number of runners. But that was not the case. According to the Fitness Products Council and American Sports Data, Inc., the number of Americans that participated in running as a fitness activity actually decreased from 32.9 million in 1987 to 32.3 million in 1997. So, the increase must have been due to an incredible change in the attitude of runners towards treadmills.

This growth in the popularity of treadmills did not stop in 1997. In 2002, a record 43.4 million runners did at least a portion of their training runs on the treadmill. While not matching the exponential growth of the 1990's, that's still a lofty 17% increase.

So, what is driving this recent surge in treadmill popularity? Could it be that runners of today are a bit less elitist? That is probably, at least partly, true. The current crop of runners is a much more diverse group. They come from many different backgrounds, have many different goals and run for many different reasons. Some are highly fit and some are not so fit. Some are world class athletes while others are just learning to run.

This diversification has been very good for the sport of running. It has made what was once a sport with low participation numbers into one of the most popular forms of exercise and competition.

The sporting goods industry took note of this and started to design treadmills that were far more user friendly. The loud and ugly machines of the past were replaced with sleek, quiet and easy to use pieces of exercise equipment. The manufacturers also added more runner friendly features, such as programmed workouts, calorie counters, elevation, and displays that made the treadmill workouts more interactive, interesting and less boring. They made the treadmills more durable, more accessible and easier to maintain.

The treadmill made it easier for a beginning runner to stick to their training program. If it was cold or dark, they could just hop on the treadmill. It took away an excuse for not running. This made the treadmill a very popular item for new runners, fitness enthusiasts and those trying to lose weight.

It was not just beginners or dieters that began to use the treadmill frequently. Experienced runners and even elite competitive runners started to incorporate treadmill runs into their training program.

I first started to run on the treadmill in the 1980's. It all started on a cold, winter day. Rather than run outside in the cold and on the ice, I ran on a treadmill at the gym. I expected to hate the treadmill workout and dreaded even starting. Then, a funny thing happened. I actually enjoyed the run! There was a television in the gym, right in front of the treadmill. It gave me a chance to get in some guilt-free television time. I was warm, comfortable and had easy access to water.

Not only was it more comfortable, but the workout was of a higher quality than I would have gotten had I tried to run on the snow and ice. I was able to concentrate on form and pace rather than focusing on my footing on the slick roads.

Shortly after that training run I purchased my first treadmill. I started to do nearly all of my "bad weather" workouts on the treadmill. At first, I defined "bad weather" as blizzard conditions. That definition soon changed. The more time I spent on the treadmill, the more I liked it and the more broad my definition of bad weather became. "Bad weather" had now become anytime the temperature was below 50 degrees. I live in Colorado, so that's half the year.

I had now become a treadmill "junkie" and I was not alone. Many top runners, including elite world class runners, now do at least some of their workouts on a treadmill.

Dr. Christine Clark is a physician and marathon runner who lives in Alaska. With two young children to care for and frigid temperatures to contend with, she turned to the treadmill for training. She did nearly all of her training on the treadmill. So, how did she do, training on the treadmill? Well, she qualified for the marathon in the Sydney Olympics with a time of 2:33:31 in the Olympic trials at Columbia, South Carolina. Not Bad!

Norwegian marathon runner, Ingrid Kristiansen, set a world record of 2:21:06 at the London Marathon in 1985. Where did she do most of her workouts during the cold Norwegian winter? You guessed it. On the treadmill.

So, I no longer hide my treadmill. I readily admit that I do a large portion of my workouts on the treadmill. I incorporate treadmill workouts into my training plan. Why? Because treadmills are for "real" runners and the benefits of treadmill running are for real.

The term "treadmill" used to bring up negative images of getting nowhere fast. That image has turned around. Today the treadmill is the most popular piece of exercise equipment available.

2

Treadmill Pros and Cons

As a running coach and a personal trainer, I get questions concerning the advantages and disadvantages of treadmill training from all types of clients. My running clients are concerned about the training effects of running on the treadmill. My personal training clients that are more interested in overall fitness and my weight loss clients have questions concerning calorie burn and health benefits.

For fitness, health and weight loss purposes, there are really no disadvantages to treadmill training. A calorie burned on a treadmill is the same as a calorie burned during any other activity. Cardiovascular fitness is improved at a similar rate whether you run on a treadmill or outside on the road or track. The treadmill provides many added benefits for this type of user including injury prevention, safety, convenience and improved exercise adherence.

The treadmill also provides these same benefits to competitive runners. Fitness gained from running on the treadmill have been shown to be very similar to training effects from free range running. In some cases treadmill training provides even greater training benefits. An example of this is the consistent pace of the treadmill. Many training programs require workouts that are performed at a precise pace and distance. The treadmill makes maintaining an exact pace and judging the precise distance much easier. You never need to guess or make assumptions concerning your distance or speed.

There are some disadvantages for competitive runners. The disadvantages are mostly related to the lack of specificity when training for road or track racing. There is a rule of training called the "rule of specificity" that says training should closely mimic the activity you are training for. There are very definite differences between treadmill running and free range running that violate this rule. Here is a summary of the pros and cons associated with treadmill running.

Pros

Adverse Weather

You look out your living room window. The wind is howling, the mercury in your thermometer is shivering at the bottom of the scale and the snow is piling up on your driveway. You have a five mile tempo run planned. Are you going to lace 'em up and head out? Unless you are about 400 meters short of a full mile, you are going to stay huddled in front of your fireplace! In situations like that a treadmill is the perfect answer. You can perform any of your training runs in the safety and comfort of your own home or at your gym.

Poor weather conditions are the bane of a distance runner's existence. There are a few die hard's out there that still enjoy running in the rain, snow and cold, but most runners, including myself, do not like it. A treadmill takes the weather factor out of the equation. You can always hop on your treadmill and do nearly any workout that you could have done outdoors. If ice or snow is present, running on the treadmill will certainly provide a better workout than running outside in those treacherous conditions.

If you're running outside on ice or snow, you must be

very cautious of your footing. It is nearly impossible to concentrate on your form or pacing when running on ice. It is also very difficult to maintain your planned pace, since you must slow down on such a slippery surface. The bulky or multi-layer clothing that you must wear in cold weather can disturb your stride and arm action.

High wind can also create havoc with your workout. Most competitive runners have a specific pace or intensity level planned for each workout. If you are running into a head wind, your pace will drop in relation to the intensity of the workout. And visa versa, if you have a tail wind your pace will be higher in relation to your intended run.

Cold weather alone will probably not adversely affect your run, but it can become an excuse not to do your planned workout. This is especially a problem for beginning runners. A treadmill removes all excuses for not running. Cold weather can also cause some breathing problems for runners with asthma. Running in a warm, climate controlled environment can help alleviate these problems.

Safety is also an issue in some weather conditions. A slip on the ice or snow can cause serious injury that could put a quick halt to your racing and training season.

Cold, ice and snow are not the only weather related problems a runner must deal with. Hot weather can create an even more serious situation. Dehydration, heat exhaustion and heat stroke are very serious conditions that are frequently encountered by runners. Each of these conditions are caused by a combination of high heat and insufficient fluids.

Running on a treadmill in a climate controlled environment with fluids readily available will take away all chances of developing these problems.

Speed Work/Interval Training

Successful interval training depends upon running your planned repeats at a fairly precise speed and for a precise distance. It is hard for most runners to accurately judge pace while training at the track and it becomes even more difficult when training on the open road. When training on the track, you at least know the exact distance you are running but on the open road it's all guesswork. There are some fairly accurate GPS training watches available that use satellite information to give you your pace and distance. These have proven to be fairly accurate, but are still not as precise as treadmill running.

When doing interval training on a treadmill, you can set the pace and be assured that you are running at that speed throughout the repeat. The treadmill does not allow you to slow down or speed up. It forces you to maintain your target pace throughout your repeat or workout.

Consistent Pacing

When you begin to fatigue during your outside training runs, you may subconsciously slow down. You do not realize that you are slowing down because you feel like you are running at the same rate of perceived exertion. In other words, you still believe that you are running at your goal pace. The accumulating effects of fatigue makes your goal pace feel harder and harder, so you slow down in response. This unintentional reduction in your pace can have a negative affect on the quality of your workout. This problem with inconsistent pace can happen in all workouts from speed work to long runs.

The treadmill will force you to maintain the pace that you had planned for your workout. The only way to slow down is to intentionally reduce the speed of the treadmill. This consistent pacing benefit can actually make treadmill training a higher quality workout than track or road training in some situations.

Easy Runs

Most competitive runners like to run fast. They love their speed work and tempo runs. But you cannot run hard and fast all of the time. Your muscles need time to rest and recover. Without that recovery time, you will not be able to complete your harder workouts at an optimal pace and quality.

Running easy is hard. In fact, running easy is one of the hardest things to do for many runners. Easy runs are necessary to allow your muscles to recover from hard, intense or long running sessions, but it can be very difficult to run at a pace easy enough to allow for muscle recovery. It can feel very slow and therefore many runners have a tendency to perform their easy runs at too fast a pace.

The treadmill fixes this problem. Once you determine your easy pace, it is a simple matter to set the treadmill at that pace and jump on. As long as you don't give into temptation and increase the speed of the machine you will stay at your easy pace for the duration of the session. Maintaining an easy pace on your rest days will allow your muscles to stay fresh and will improve the quality of your harder training runs and avoid overtraining problems.

How easy should your easy runs be?. One rule of thumb is the "talk test". As you are running you should be able to speak clearly, but not sing.

Beginning runners can also benefit by using the treadmill for easy runs. It is important for a new runner to strengthen seldom used tendons and muscles gradually before doing any intense or fast training. Setting the treadmill at an easy pace will help avoid any tendency to run faster than they should.

Hill Training

Hill running is one of the best and most efficient workouts for building running strength, running economy and improving race performance. The problem is that many runners are hill challenged. They live in areas that have few hills, if any. So, what do you do if you live in a hill challenged area? Simple - get on your treadmill. Most treadmills will elevate from 1 percent to 12 percent. Some elevate as high as 15% or more. There are some newer models that also decline 2 or 3 percent, which would be great training for races with some downhill sections such as the Boston Marathon or trail races. The elevation selections will allow you to closely mimic nearly any outside trail or road race.

Even if you have access to hills in your area the nearly unlimited variety of possible hill workouts on your treadmill will give you a greater variety of hill training options.

The treadmill not only supplies hills to those without hills, it also removes hills for those that don't want them. Many runners that live in mountain communities have problems finding a route that does not have hills. There are many times, especially during easy runs and periods of rest and recovery, that you do not want to run on hills. The treadmill will flatten the most hilly terrain!

Long Runs

The term long run brings up visions of running long distances in parks, on roads or urban trails. There are many great benefits of doing long runs on that type of terrain. However, more and more runners are doing at least some of their long runs on the treadmill. Many do all of their winter long runs on the treadmill to avoid weather related problems.

Running on a treadmill for two or three hours sounds boring. But for that matter so is running outside for long periods of time. When doing long runs on the treadmill you can watch television or listen to music to help alleviate boredom. I like to tape marathons or other running events and watch them while I run. I also enjoy watching running movies. Any movie will entertain you while you run, but I find that running movies keep me motivated.

The quality of your long runs can also be improved by running on the treadmill. The precise pace control will allow you to keep the pace down when necessary. It will keep you from running too fast during the first part of your long run. It will also keep you at a quality pace if you are doing goal pace long runs. It can be very difficult to maintain that quality goal pace in the later stages of your long run. The treadmill will keep you at that goal pace and you don't even have to think about it. This is essential for marathon training. During the last 6 to 8 miles of a marathon, it becomes very difficult to maintain your pace. In order to run your best marathon, you should practice maintaining your goal pace when you are very fatigued. Since the treadmill does not get tired, you must push the button to slow it down. So, the machine will keep you on your pace unless you make the decision to reduce your speed.

When doing your long runs on a treadmill, you are also near all of your water and fluid replacement drinks. No need to hide fluids in a bush or carry them with you. You are also just steps from a bathroom. No more quick trips behind the bushes.

Injury Prevention/Rehabilitation

Running on concrete and asphalt day in and day out places a lot of stress on the connective tissues, joints and muscles in your legs. This can lead to potential overuse injuries.

High quality treadmills that are produced today give you a stable but more forgiving surface. Treadmills are available in a fairly wide range of surface "softness". The firmness of the treadmill is determined by a combination of the running deck and the suspension system. Some are designed to more closely mimic the firm asphalt or concrete surface of the road and others are designed with a lot of "give" in order to provide a very soft ride for heavy runners or those with injury problems. There are even some machines available that are adjustable to different levels of shock absorption.

Programmed Workouts

Most quality treadmills have pre-programmed workouts that are designed for anything from weight loss to 10K races. This feature makes it easy for runners that are not interested in designing their own program.

For those that do develop their own training programs, many treadmills have the ability to store custom workouts. You just manually adjust the treadmill as you run. The treadmill will "remember" the workout. The next time you do that workout the treadmill makes all of the adjustments automatically. Some of the newer, high tech treadmills even have the ability to download custom workouts over the internet.

When rehabilitating an injury it is important to add stress to the injured area very gradually. The softer running surface makes treadmill a superior method of rehabilitation.

Mental Toughness

The sport of running is a solitary activity that requires self-motivation, discipline and commitment along with both physical and mental toughness. These are all attributes that must be learned and practiced.

Running on a treadmill is comfortable, efficient and safe. But, it is not psychologically easy. It is really quite difficult to run and maintain pace on a treadmill. This is due, in part, to the perception that you are not going anywhere. You do not have the psychological cues that you are making progress, such as the wind in your face and the objects and scenery moving by. You also do not have other runners around you to keep you motivated.

Since running on the treadmill is usually a solitary activity it helps build self-motivation and commitment. Running and maintaining your pace on the treadmill builds a mental "toughness" that will help you in your races and outside training runs.

Great For Beginners

The treadmill is ideal for beginning runners. Many new runners feel a bit intimidated by the sport and by more experienced runners. There is no reason for them to feel this way but many do none the less. The treadmill gives these beginners a great place to start and to gain confidence in themselves so that feeling of intimidation melts away.

Most new runners start with walking. The treadmill is a great tool for incorporating those first running steps into a training program. It is very easy to add in very short surges of running. The treadmill provides them with a stable, level and dry surface in which to practice those first running steps.

The information provided by the display, such as time, speed, calories burned and distance traveled are all great motivational tools for beginners.

Heart Rate Training

Training by heart rate is a currently popular method of monitoring running intensity. Many mid and top range treadmills have built in heart rate monitoring capabilities. Some monitor heart rate by using a belt that wraps around your chest and others use monitoring pads on the treadmill handle grips.

A very useful function incorporated into some high end treadmills, is a program that regulates the treadmill speed and incline according to your heart rate. You simply tell the treadmill what your target heart rate range is. If your heart rate drops below your target range the treadmill either speeds up or increases it's incline. If you rise above your target heart rate the treadmill decreases it's speed or it's incline in response.

This is an essential feature for those that are running to rehabilitate after an illness, surgery or injury. Doctors often prescribe exercise performed at a specific heart rate. Heart rate feedback will keep these individuals exercising at the proper intensity.

Workout Variety

Treadmill workouts have an unlimited number of possible combinations of speed, distance and incline. You are able to design a run that will provide you with the exact workout that you desire. There is no outside training area that can give you everything you want in a workout. Only the treadmill gives you this kind of flexibility. This is an advantage to runners of all abilities, from a beginner to an elite runner.

Running Feedback

The console of today's treadmills give you a wealth of information. They tell you the distance you traveled, speed, average speed, calories burned, heart rate, pace and incline. This feedback provides you with important training information, training records and is also a motivational tool.

Air Pollution

Running outdoors in an area of high air pollution can be hazardous. Air pollution can come from automobile traffic, industrial exhaust, wood or coal burning or even forest fires. You should avoid running outside during times of high air pollution, especially if you suffer from asthma or any other respiratory problem.

Check air quality reports in your local paper. You can also check the current Air Quality Index (AQI) on the internet at www.epa.gov/airnow. If the readings are 100 to 150, sensitive individuals can be adversely affected. If it is over 150 outside running can be hazardous for everyone. Running indoors on the treadmill is the ideal answer when you encounter these types of conditions.

Cons

The treadmill provides many benefits. But, as with everything, it is not perfect. Along with its many advantages, the treadmill does have some disadvantages.

Law of Specificity

One of the "laws" of training is the law of specificity. This simply means that your training should be as specific as possible to your training goal. In other words, your training should match your goal as closely as possible. You are training to run outside on the road, trail or track and run races, not to run on a treadmill.

Treadmill training has been proven, in scientific studies, to have very similar physiological effects, to outside or free-range running. In simpler terms, treadmill training gives you very similar training benefits when compared to free-range running. However, even though the physiological effects are very similar, it is not specifically the same as running outside. There are physical differences, which include lack of wind resistance, lack of changing

> *The training law of specificity states that your training should match your goal. This is the main reason that you should do some of your workouts on the road or track.*

terrain, running on a moving belt, bio-mechanical differences and psychological differences.

Lack of Wind Resistance

When running on the treadmill you are obviously running in place. You're not running through the air. When you run outside you are running through the molecules of the air which create resistance. The faster you run the more of an effect the air resistance has on you. Studies have estimated that air resistance creates an increase in your running workload of between 2% and 10%, depending upon your running speed. The faster you run, the more of an effect the wind resistance has. This problem is simple to overcome. You can compensate for the wind resistance by simply elevating your treadmill one percent.

Running Bio-Mechanics

In addition to the wind resistance problem, there is some evidence that running bio-mechanics are different when running on the treadmill. There have been very few conclusive studies done on the running form differences between treadmill and free range running. The studies that have been done have presented some rather conflicting data. Here is a brief summary of the reported running mechanics problems that have been associated with treadmill running.

- **Stride Length** - Many runners use a treadmill stride length that is either longer and shorter than outside running. One study on the effects of treadmill running came up with some very interesting data. The study used one group of subjects that were very experienced runners and compared them to a group of new runners. The results showed that the more experienced group had longer strides when running on the treadmill, compared to their same pace when running outside. The interesting part is that the inexperienced group had the exact opposite result. They had shorter stride lengths on the treadmill than they did when running outside. More research is needed to determine why this happens and if it happens consistently to a large group of runners.

- **Longer Support Time** - Support time is the amount of time that your support leg spends on the ground. Some runners tend to spend more time on their support leg when running on the treadmill. In order to maximize your running efficiency your support time should be kept at a minimum. If your support leg is on the ground longer, you are probably not running as efficiently as you could be. This increase in support time is probably caused by an unconscious desire to provide a more stable running base on the moving and somewhat unstable treadmill.

- **Less Forward Lean** - Some studies have determined that some athletes run with less of a forward lean when running on the treadmill. This can cause more energy being wasted on up and down motion and less energy focused on forward momentum. Less forward lean can also contribute to over striding.

Running Surface

The even and soft surface of the treadmill is an advantage in many ways but it does present one major disadvantage. When running outside you encounter uneven surfaces, stones, soft areas, hard areas, dry areas, wet areas and various combinations of these surfaces. The challenge of running over these surfaces improves your propreoception or the ability of your neuromuscular system to correct for the effect these types of surfaces have on your muscles and the position of your body parts and joints. This is critical to runners because it affects balance, power and running economy. Running on the treadmill removes this very important part of training.

Psychological Differences

Psychology plays a large role in the performance of runners. Treadmill running has several psychological factors that can affect the benefits of treadmill training.

- **Lack of Visual Cues** - When running outside you are moving past trees, buildings, automobiles and other people. When you are on the treadmill, you are not moving so you do not have those visual cues that signify movement. This can be very disconcerting and can lead to problems with running mechanics, confidence and training adherence.
- **Perception of Limited Room** - A properly fitted treadmill gives you more that sufficient room for even the longest running strides. However, the limited size of the running surface of the treadmill can give the impression that you may either "run off" the front of the machine or "fall off" the back. This commonly leads to a shortened and/or more vertical stride.
- **Lack of Confidence** - Many runners, especially more experienced runners that have been training most of their lives on the open road, do not trust the training benefits of treadmill running. This can be a self full filling prophecy. If you do not believe in something, it can and probably will have a negative effect on its benefits.
- **Boredom** - This is the daddy of all mental hurdles of treadmill training. Running in place can be boring and tedious. But take heart. This one is easily overcome.

Availability of Gym Treadmills

If you don't have your own treadmill and choose to use one at a gym there is the problem of availability. Treadmills are very popular in a gym and it can be hard to find one not in use. When you do find one, there is usually a time limit of around 30 minutes per person so you may not be able to do long workouts. The best way to solve this is to go to the gym during off hours. If there is no one waiting in line to use the treadmill you can usually stay on the machine as long as you want.

Accuracy

As I mentioned earlier, the workouts on a treadmill can be more precise than outside running because you can monitor exactly how fast and how far you are running. But, that is assuming that your treadmill is calibrated accurately. Treadmills are notorious for being delivered from the factory with poor calibration. Most treadmill manufactures do not pay a lot of attention to exact accuracy. They don't believe that most users will notice the inaccuracy and many do not care. So, they don't put a lot of their resources into insuring accuracy. This is more of a problem with low end treadmills. The makes of high end treadmill pay much more attention to those types of details in their machines.

It doesn't take much of an error to make a big difference in your training. An error of just 10% can create problems. A 7:00 pace on an inaccurate treadmill could actually be a 7:15 pace. An error of this size can totally change the result and quality of your training run.

A good technician can calibrate your treadmill for you and it is well worth the money. If you just bought a treadmill have it checked. The manufacturer warranty will cover the cost of calibration of any high quality treadmill.

Here is an easy way to check the accuracy of your treadmill. To do this you need to know the length of your running belt. Get the information from your treadmill manufacturer. If you can't find the information you will need to measure the belt. You need the length of the entire belt including the part wrapping around the rollers.

Divide 2,112 by the length of your belt in inches. This will give you how many complete revolutions the belt should make in one minute at 2 MPH.

Now place a small piece of bright tape on the belt. Start

the treadmill and take it up to 2 MPH. Count the number of revolutions the belt makes. For every one revolution higher or lower, the treadmill speed is off by .1MPH.

Here is an example: If your treadmill belt is 100 inches long - 2112/100 = 21.12. If you counted 23 revolutions in 1 minute, your treadmill speed is about .2 MPH too fast.

Cost

Quality treadmills are not cheap. You can buy lower end treadmills at a discount store for $500 or less. But, this type of treadmill will not stand up to the abuse that a runner puts on it. It will also not operate smoothly, will not be as accurate, will be noisier and just not be an enjoyable experience.

A quality treadmill will start at around $1000 and go up to over $8000 for a club quality machine. This is a lot of money but if you are going to use your treadmill on a consistent basis it will be worth the extra cost to get a quality machine. You can usually find a good used treadmill in the classified ads. A good time to buy is in the several months after the New Year. Many people buy treadmills as a New Years resolution. They use them one or two times and then give up. You can usually pick one up for a bargain price. Also check with fitness specialty retail stores. Some of these shops will take used treadmills as trade ins or may have a treadmill returned by dissatisfied buyer. These machines can be purchased at discount prices.

3

Common Treadmill Pitfalls

Running on a treadmill is a overall positive experience, but there are a number of minor problems associated with treadmill running. Some are built in problems that can't be avoided and will affect all runners. Others are simply bad habits that can be corrected or warded off with sufficient practice and mental focus.

Treadmill Equivalent Pace

As I mentioned earlier, the moving belt and the fact that you are not traveling forward against the force of air, makes treadmill running a bit easier than outside running. You are running over a moving surface rather than propelling yourself along a static surface. In order to make treadmill running more comparable to free range running you can simply elevate your treadmill to 1 percent. How about steeper inclines? How does do they affect your treadmill equivalent pace? The following table is a chart that gives you an estimate of the free range running equivalent of treadmill paces at various inclines. Keep in mind that these are rough approximations. The equations involve a lot of assumptions, but should be fairly close for most runners. I would not suggest using elevations over 2% to mimic running on a flat road. The equivalent paces given for elevations of 3% and higher will give you the equivalent pace in terms of intensity and effort, but it becomes more of a hill workout and does not sufficiently match flat road running.

Equivalent Free Range Pace With Various Incline Settings in Minutes Per Mile						
Pace	0%	1%	2%	3%	4%	5%
5:00	5:21	5:06	4:53	4:41	4:29	4:19
5:10	5:32	5:17	5:03	4:50	4:38	4:27
5:20	5:43	5:27	5:12	4:59	4:47	4:36
5:30	5:53	5:37	5:22	5:09	4:56	4:45
5:40	6:04	5:47	5:32	5:18	5:05	4:53
5:50	6:15	5:58	5:42	5:27	5:14	5:02
6:00	6:26	6:08	5:52	5:37	5:23	5:11
6:10	6:36	6:18	6:01	5:46	5:32	5:19
6:20	6:47	6:28	6:11	5:55	5:41	5:28
6:30	6:58	6:38	6:21	6:05	5:50	5:36
6:40	7:08	6:49	6:31	6:14	5:59	5:45
6:50	7:19	6:59	6:40	6:24	6:08	5:54
7:00	7:30	7:09	6:50	6:33	6:17	6:02
7:10	7:41	7:19	7:00	6:42	6:26	6:11
7:20	7:51	7:30	7:10	6:52	6:35	6:20
7:30	8:02	7:40	7:20	7:01	6:44	6:28
7:40	8:13	7:50	7:29	7:10	6:53	6:37
7:50	8:24	8:00	7:39	7:20	7:02	6:46
8:00	8:34	8:11	7:49	7:29	7:11	6:54
8:10	8:45	8:21	7:59	7:39	7:20	7:03
8:20	8:56	8:31	8:08	7:48	7:29	7:11
8:30	9:06	8:41	8:18	7:57	7:38	7:20

Equivalent Free Range Pace With Various Incline Settings in Minutes Per Mile						
Pace	0%	1%	2%	3%	4%	5%
8:40	9:17	8:51	8:28	8:07	7:47	7:29
8:50	9:28	9:02	8:38	8:16	7:56	7:37
9:00	9:39	9:12	8:48	8:25	8:05	7:46
9:20	10:00	9:32	9:07	8:44	8:23	8:03
9:40	10:21	9:53	9:27	9:03	8:41	8:21
10:00	10:43	10:13	9:46	9:22	8:59	8:38
10:20	11:04	10:34	10:06	9:40	9:17	8:55
10:40	11:26	10:54	10:25	9:59	9:35	9:12
11:00	11:47	11:15	10:45	10:18	9:53	9:30
11:20	12:09	11:35	11:05	10:37	10:11	9:47
11:40	12:30	11:56	11:24	10:55	10:29	10:04
12:00	12:52	12:16	11:44	11:14	10:47	10:22

Running Form and Mechanics

The mechanics involved in running on the tread-mill are a bit different than when running outside. During free range running you are pushing off against the ground and generating your own forward momentum. When running on the treadmill the belt is moving underneath you while you maintain your position in the air above the belt. This is a substantial difference

Treadmill running is a good opportunity to work on your running form. Since you don't need to worry about traffic or debris you are free to concentrate fully on your stride. If possible, place a mirror along a wall so you can see your form and make any necessary adjustments.

and can be the cause of changes in your running form and biomechanics.

One of the objectives of treadmill training is to run using the same form and mechanics as when running outside. If you start to allow form flaws to appear when treadmill training, it could adversely affect all of your training runs and your racing performance. So, it's critical, in the case of competitive runners, to run on the treadmill using the same stride and mechanics you use when running outside. This is a bit less important for fitness or recreational runners, but it is still something you should consider because running with different mechanics on the treadmill could possibly lead to injury. The possible form flaws on the treadmill are very similar to free range running form problems. They include:

- **Too much vertical movement** - The moving belt can cause you to run too upright and bouncy. A lot of energy is wasted with up and down motions. All of your energy and momentum should be directed forward, with a very slight total body forward lean. There should not be a forward lean at the waist. Your body should remain straight and relaxed with a slight total body forward lean. Your stride should be smooth and low to the ground with little wasted motion.

- **Leaning forward at the waist** - Some runners subconsciously try to lean excessively forward and push against the belt. You do want to have a strong push off, but it should be a quick, natural push off. You should not be trying to force the belt backwards. Try to ignore the fact that you are running over a moving surface. Visualize running outside and floating over the pavement or trail. Always concentrate on maintaining your normal running stride.

- **Pawing back excessively** - This is another treadmill form flaw that is usually a subconscious action. There is a tendency to feel like you need to keep up with the moving belt. This can result in a "pawing back" motion in which you pull your lead leg force-fully back under your body. This results in poor running economy, excessive energy usage and breaks your forward momentum. It can also be the cause of a short stride. Concentrate on keeping all of your momentum and energy moving forward. Allow your body to "float" over your front foot as it comes down directly under your center of gravity.

- **Understriding** - The limited length of the belt can be a strong psychological barrier. Many runners feel somewhat claustrophobic on the treadmill. They may feel like they do not have room to run with their normal relaxed, smooth stride. They run with a cramped, tight and short running style that is inefficient for distance running. If you run in the center of the belt you have plenty of room for your normal stride. This problem is more common with new treadmill users. As confidence increases, this problem usually corrects itself. One word of caution here. If you are a tall runner with very long legs, make sure you purchase a treadmill with a long deck. A combination of long legs and a short deck can be a bad combination. Do not run too close to the front of the treadmill. Running too close to the front of the machine can cause problems with both your leg action and your arm swing. If you run close to the front, your natural arm swing can cause you to hit the frame or console of the treadmill with your hands. This will lead to a shortened arm swing, a low arm swing or a high arm swing with hunched, tense shoulders. Make sure you run far enough back to allow for a free arm swing. Running too far forward can also cause you to hit the cowling at the front of the treadmill with your feet, which can cause stride inefficiencies and stumbling.

- **Overstriding** - There can also be a tendency to over-stride when running on the treadmill. This is another subconscious problem that is caused by a desire to overcome the movement of the belt. Follow good form guidelines - pushing off, directing all momentum and energy forward and float over your lead foot as it lands under your center of gravity. Do not reach out with your forward foot. If you reach too far forward with your lead foot, you will land heavily on your heel. This will result in an inefficient "braking" action on each step.

Visualization and focus will help you avoid and fix these treadmill form problems. When you are running on the treadmill, try to forget that you are on a moving belt. Visualize yourself running on the roads. Put the moving belt out of your mind and create a mental image of propelling yourself smoothly forward along a trail, road or track. When your treadmill is elevated, don't dwell on the fact that you are running on a tilted deck. Visualize a hill in front of you and attack the hill with the same mechanics that you have always used for your hill work.

Recent studies have found that thinking about an activity produces the same activity as the actual activity. This process of visualization can help you improve your stride mechanics, run smoother and with less effort.

It takes some practice, but soon you will forget you are on a machine and your treadmill workouts will be more efficient and enjoyable.

Hanging On

There is an almost irresistible urge to hold on to the handles or railing of the treadmill when you are running. This especially becomes a problem when you start to fatigue or when running on an elevated treadmill. Even the fastest and most experienced treadmill runners will occasionally fight a battle of will to avoid grabbing onto the handles.

This is a problem that, if allowed to get started, can become progressively worse and become a very hard habit to break. So, the best advice is don't start. If you feel the urge to grab on, just imagine that the handles or railings are red hot. I still have the bad habit of reaching out to the handles once in a while. As soon as I touch them I come to my senses and pull my hands back like I was burned.

Focus on your running form and bio-mechanics. Especially pay attention to your arm actions. Keep your upper body soft and relaxed with a steady pumping motion with your arms. Keep you arm motion compact. Drive your elbows back and do not reach out in front of your body with your arms. Keep up your visualizations of floating along a trail or road. In time, this will become second nature and you will soon forget about those tempting handles and railings.

What do you do if you already have developed this bad treadmill habit? You need to break it. You probably won't be able to break the habit cold turkey. It will take some time. Try setting a goal of time or distance that you will not hang on. If you're holding on most of the time you will most likely need to set short goals. Try to run for either 2 minutes or 1/4 mile without holding on. Do not let yourself grab the handles for that amount of time. Once you are fairly comfortable with that amount of time, increase it. Keep doing this until you are able to complete your entire workout without hanging on. Of course, if you only grab the handles a few times during your workout, you can probably break the habit quickly. Try to do your whole workout without touching the handles. You will really have to concentrate on this for several workouts until you really get this handle monster beaten.

Does it really matter if you hold on? You bet it does. Hanging on to the treadmill while you run has several adverse affects.

- **It alters your form and mechanics** - When you hang on to the front or sides of the treadmill you are changing the posture of your body. You are either leaning forward into the treadmill and pushing or you are leaning backward against the resistance of the treadmill resulting in a "sitting in the bucket" position in which you are bouncing excessively up and down. You are no longer pushing off properly and "floating" over your support leg. You begin to let the moving belt guide your feet and legs. Your lack of arm motion completely throws off the symmetry of your stride. Your breathing is no longer synchronized with your stride. This is not only bad for your training, it can also cause injury. During a normal running stride, there is rotation at the hips. Part of this is the result of upper body rotation. When you hold on, you are stabilizing your upper body, This forces your hips to over-rotate in order to compensate, which can cause hip, knee, back and even ankle injury.
- **It reduces the intensity of the workout** - By holding on to the treadmill, you are letting the machine do more of the work. Your legs are just going along for the ride. This is especially true when doing hill work. It is like hanging onto a rope and having someone pull you along. If improving running performance is your goal, this is totally counter-productive.
- **It makes you mentally weaker** - Running requires a lot of mental toughness. Part of the purpose of training is to improve your mental fortitude. A major benefit of treadmill running is that it will increase your psychological toughness even more than free range running - IF YOU DO NOT HOLD ON. Holding on has the opposite effect. It is giving into a weakness, which is something that a competitive runner cannot do.

Stepping Off

Another nasty treadmill habit that can develop is stepping off the machine when you become fatigued. The treadmill can give you a superior workout due to the fact that you cannot slow down unless you slow the machine down. When running outside it is very common to slow your pace when you become fatigued. That does not happen with treadmill training unless you consciously make the decision to slow down the belt. But, there is something that you can do when you get fatigued. You can step off the machine or you can turn it off.

If you cannot stop yourself from stepping off or stopping the treadmill before your workout is finished, you may be running faster than your fitness level allows. It is better to complete your workout at a slower pace than to run faster than you should and acquire the habit of not completing your training run.

Since stepping off the treadmill requires a conscious decision, it is a less common problem than hanging on, which can happen on impulse. Beginning runners, that have not yet developed the mental conditioning that veteran runners have, will experience this problem more often than an experienced athlete.

Many beginners will step off the treadmill to get a drink, change the channel on the television, wipe their face, etc. In most cases this is just an excuse to stop for a few minutes. Don't allow yourself to get into this habit. As a beginning runner, you should start to develop that mental toughness that is so important in running and life. There are, of course, legitimate reasons for stopping. If you ever feel dizzy, disoriented or are having any type of pain, you should stop exercising.

A few years ago, I discovered a valid reason for stopping, the hard way. I began to get overheated while I was running on my treadmill. I decided to try to remove my shirt while I was running along on the machine. I got the shirt half way over my head and lost my balance. After doing a tap dance on the running belt for a few seconds, I found myself flying backwards through the air and slammed into a wall. From that point on I stop running when I want to take my shirt off. So, the point is you should always stop running if health or safety is in question. But, if you are stopping because you are struggling mentally, try to work through it. It will provide you with valuable mental and physical toughness training.

This habit is not reserved only for treadmill training. Some free range runners also do this. They obviously do not step off a machine, but they simply stop running when they get tired. As your mental toughness improves with training, this problem should take care of itself.

If you have a habit of doing this and cannot break the cycle, follow the same suggestions that were given for breaking the habit of hanging on. Set small goals of time or distance. Do not let yourself step off until you meet that goal. Then gradually increase your goal time or distance until you are performing your entire workout without stepping off the machine.

Some athletes leave the treadmill running when they step off. This is a bad practice, not only safety reasons, but because the data continues to add up miles, minutes and calories burned. If you do not turn off the machine when you are not running, you will not have accurate feedback. So, make sure you turn off the machine before you step off. Most treadmills have a pause feature. It will save your data and allow you to continue on from where you stopped with no data loss.

4

Treadmill Buyers Guide

Treadmills were the hottest piece of home exercise equipment in the 1990's and this trend appears to be continuing into the 2000's. According to the Fitness Products Council around $1.5 billion was spent on treadmills in 1997 alone.

There is good reason for this trend. Treadmills burn more calories per hour than any other piece of exercise equipment. A study completed by the Journal of the American Medical Association (JAMA) showed that a fairly vigorous workout on a treadmill burns around 700 calories, compared to 627 for stair climbers and 498 for stationary bikes.

Treadmills also require very little skill to operate. The walking or running motion is natural. You need only a good pair of shoes and you are ready to go. You can adjust the intensity of your exercise from very easy to maximal effort.

The drawback is cost. The cost of a high quality treadmill will range from just under $1000 to $9000 for a top quality commercial grade treadmill. There are treadmills available for $500 and under, but for the most part, these low-end machines are unreliable and will not stand up to consistent use. A competitive or serious recreational runner that plans on doing some of their training on a treadmill should purchase a heavy duty treadmill that will stand up to the consistent use, including 2 to 4 hour long runs. Here are some tips on features and specifications that will hopefully make your shopping experience easier and more successful.

Motors

Horsepower

Horsepower is a measure of the amount of power a motor has. Horsepower ratings can be determined by peak performance, intermediate duty or continuous duty. You should look for the continuous duty rating. This is the rating of the motor, with a significant workload and continuous and steady use. You will want a motor with at least 1.5 continuous-duty horsepower.

It is important for runners to choose a treadmill that has a powerful continuous-duty rating. Confirm this by running on the machine before you buy. When you step onto the machine, it should not bog down, slow down or show signs of struggling.

It would be preferable to have at least 2.0 continuous duty horsepower if you are going to use the treadmill consistently or if you are a competitive runner or serious recreational runner.

Some manufacturers will list a high peak-performance rating. Beware of that type of rating. It shows the motors maximum power, not its sustained output. A motor with high peak power may not be able to produce the horsepower needed to sustain a consistent output when a user is running on the treadmill, especially when using the incline. This can result in a treadmill that bogs down or slows with each step and will not give you a smooth ride. So, be sure to check for continuous duty rating. You will find treadmills that range from 1 horsepower to 3 horsepower. Even in the case of an acceptable continuous duty rating, make sure you check out the motor carefully, because there is no established method of rating motors among treadmill manufacturers.

A high quality motor must be combined with high quality electronics and construction. The electronics of the treadmill should sense the load on the motor and make adjustments automatically to keep the belt turning at a consistent and accurate speed. When you test the treadmill, watch out for any hesitation or fluctuation in the belt speed when you are walking or running on it. Any fluctuation can indicate poor quality electronics or poor communication between the motor and its controller.

Industrial grade motors carry ratings of A,B,C,F or H. Motors rated A,B or C are lower grade motors. Look for motors with a rating of F or H. This grade of motor is larger and has superior ventilation. As a result the motor will run cooler and last longer.

Controller

Power controller boards control treadmill motors. This regulates the currents that are sent to the motor. The most commonly used types of controllers are known as PWM (Pulse Width Modulated) or SCR (Solid State Control Rectifier). While both will get the job done, PWM boards are the preferred type because they produce less heat and draw fewer amps, which will result in longer motor life and fewer service calls. A PWM board will also produce more power and run quieter. All high quality treadmills should use a PWM board.

Deck

The belt and deck are the two items that will need consistent maintenance and will require periodic replacement throughout the life of your treadmill. For this reason, you should choose a deck and belt that is of high quality. With treadmills, you get what you pay for, so expect to pay more for high quality components. Consider a reversible deck. When one side wears out, you can flip it around. This will double the life of your running deck.

The deck of the treadmill is the bed of the treadmill that the belt moves over. Consumers often overlook this, perhaps because it is hidden under the belt.

A high quality deck will be pretreated with a lubricant of some type to minimize friction. This type of deck will usually require very little maintenance on the part of the consumer.

Even with consistent maintenance, the deck will eventually wear out over time. This is due to the friction between the bottom surface of the running belt and the top of the deck. Some decks are reversible, meaning they can be turned over resulting in double the life of a non-reversible deck. This would be a good feature to look for if you plan on doing a lot of your workouts on the treadmill. It will double the life of your deck.

Excessive friction between the deck and the belt is a cause of malfunction and breakdown. For this reason it is important to choose a deck that minimizes friction between the deck and the belt. Avoid any deck that does not have some sort of pretreating such as silicone or a permanent wax.

Belts

Belts are another part of the treadmill that will wear out and eventually need to be replaced. Belts can be single ply or two ply. Generally, two-ply belts are of higher quality. The belt should lay flat on the deck. There should not be any curling on the edges of the belt. If you notice curling or fraying on the sides of the belt, you should investigate further. It may be a sign of a poor quality belt.

Rollers

The running belt wraps around the rollers at the front and back of the treadmill. They place tension on the belt and keep it moving smoothly and accurately.

Look for a treadmill with a roller size of 2 inches or more. These larger rollers allow the belt to be adjusted with less tension, which increases the life of the belt and bearings. The decreased tension will allow the system to operate at a cooler temperature because the load on the bearings, motor and controller are lessened. Another good feature is a crowned roller in which the center is wider than the ends. This helps keep the belt running in the center of the treadmill.

Frame

Look for a heavy-duty frame that is constructed of high alloy steel. This type of frame is heavier than aluminum, but is more durable and stable. A lighter weight frame will not be as stable and may not stand up to heavy use. The treadmill is an expensive and long term investment, so make sure you purchase one that will last a long time.

It is a great convenience to have rollers on the heavy, motor end of the treadmill. This will make relocation and moving for cleaning much easier. Without rollers, it will take two or three strong backs to move these heavy machines.

Welded frames will generally be more stable over time. A bolted frame has a tendency to "shake loose" and will require more frequent maintenance. A welded frame will also be quieter with less shakes and rattles.

Control Console

You will want a computerized control panel that will tell you, at a minimum, your speed, pace, distance and time. Other useful features to look for are average speed, average pace, calories burned, calories burned per hour and heart rate.

Look for a console that is easy to read and that has control buttons that are convenient and easy to reach. Price will usually go up as you get more features and programs on the control panel. Look for the features that will keep you most interested in your workout.

Some treadmills have an emergency off button on the console. Check the placement of this off button. Some of them are located in a place that you can accidentally hit while you are running. It is really annoying to have the treadmill shut down in the middle of your workout.

Cushioning

Choose the level of cushioning carefully. If you primarily train for road racing, you will want a firmer ride. If you are more interested in weight loss or fitness, a more cushioned machine will be more appropriate.

An advantage to running on treadmills is that they are generally cushioned to reduce the impact of running. Manufacturers use different methods of cushioning, including shock absorption suspensions and flexible decks or frames.

You do not want a treadmill with too much flexibility. If it is excessively bouncy or cushioned it can have an adverse effect on your joints. It can be like trying to run in soft sand if it is too soft.

How much cushioning you want will depend on your goals. If you are using the treadmill to train for road racing, you will want minimal cushioning in order to more closely mimic outdoor running. If overall fitness is your goal, a little more cushioning will help protect your joints. You will also want a softer ride if you have injury problems. Try out several different treadmills to get a feel for what you like.

There are some newer, high end models that have adjustable levels of cushioning. This can be a very valuable tool for the multi-user environment. Even a single user will draw some benefit from an adjustable model. You could use the softer setting during recovery periods or when rehabilitating an injury, and the firmer settings for more race specific training.

Incline

You will want a treadmill with the ability to incline. All high quality treadmills will have this feature. Most treadmills will start at a 1 degree incline and go up to 10 or 12 degrees. Some high-end treadmills will also decline, which is a handy feature for training for hilly road races where there is a lot of downhill running.

The method of incline varies from treadmill to treadmill. Possible methods include hand crank, powered screws, electric rack and pinion motors and pneumatic shocks. The most common and preferred method is electric rack and pinion motors.

The most important thing to watch out for is the stability of the treadmill when inclined. All treadmills will be a bit less stable when at full incline, but there should not be excessive instability.

Speed

Most treadmills have a speed range of 1 MPH to 10 MPH. There are some high-end treadmills that will go up to 12 MPH. Some very expensive commercial treadmills have an even higher speed. These treadmills are usually used for research purposes or by professional sports teams for high speed training. These specialty treadmills can become extremely expensive.

Only individuals that are using the treadmill to train for competitive road racing will need speeds as high as 12 MPH. If you are a fitness runner and do not plan to train for road racing, a machine that tops out at 10 MPH will be sufficient. If you are looking for a treadmill with 12 MPH capability, be aware that some require 220-volt circuits. In recent years, more and more manufacturers have been producing machines that go up to 12 MPH and only require a 110-volt circuit. This is a sign of the increasing demand for quality treadmills, by competitive runners. But keep in mind that some of them still require a 220-volt circuit. So shop carefully. It can be expensive to upgrade your wiring to include a 220-volt outlet for your treadmill.

When shopping for a treadmill, try to plan ahead. You may only need a treadmill that goes up to 10MPH today. But what if you improve your fitness to a level at which you need a faster machine? It will be cheaper in the long run to purchase for the future now.

Starting speed is an important safety consideration. Starting speeds of more that 1 MPH can make it difficult to safely mount the treadmill. Most high quality treadmills will not have that problem, but keep it in mind, especially if you are a beginning runner.

Many lower end treadmills, that are designed for walking, will have a high speed of 8 MPH. If you are only going to walk on the treadmill, 8 MPH is a sufficiently high speed.

If you think that you may decide to use the treadmill for running, you should purchase one that has a top speed of at least 10 MPH. Always try to think ahead. If you believe that you may want to run on the treadmill at some point, it will be more cost effective to buy a runners treadmill now rather than have to upgrade in the future.

If you want a treadmill to use for sprint distance training, there is one available. It is the A.R. Young high speed treadmill. This machine will go at a blistering 26+ MPH!. This treadmill is very expensive and use of this treadmill requires a spotter (someone to grab you if you are thrown off the treadmill).

Size

The size of the treadmill is an important individual consideration. The belt must be long enough to accommodate your longest possible stride with some room left over. You do not want to try to run on a treadmill that you feel you may step off of when you are exercising.

The belt should be at least 50 inches long and preferably at least 55 to 60 inches for taller users. The width should be no less than 16 or 17 inches. 18 inches or more would be preferable. You should not

The length of the running area is the most important size consideration. A running belt that is too short can cause you to feel cramped and uncomfortable. This can result in stride problems and a decrease in the quality of your workout.

have to worry that you will step off the back of the treadmill and should not be stepping on the front cowling. If you feel too cramped on the machine, it can cause you to change your stride.

Heart rate monitor and control

There are a number of methods used for monitoring heart rate, including chest straps, ear clips, finger clips and hand contact monitors. The most accurate are the chest strap monitors.

Ear and finger tip monitors tend to shake loose when you are running and can give a faulty reading. There are some units that operate with a hand grip. You simply grab onto the hand grip when you wish to take a reading. This system works well when walking, but is difficult and sometimes inaccurate when running.

Heart rate monitors will give you constant feedback concerning your heart rate. Some treadmills are offering a control feature which will vary the incline or speed of the treadmill automatically in order to keep your heart rate at a pre-determined level. If your heart rate strays above or below a pre-set range, either the incline or speed will adjust automatically.

Safety

There are a number of safety feature that are available. Select the ones that are most appropriate for your needs. If you have small children in your household, there are safety keys available. The treadmill will not operate without the key inserted. There is also a strap on the key, which can be attached to your body, so if you fall or are thrown from the treadmill, the key will turn off the treadmill.

Some treadmills have emergency off buttons. Check to make sure that the emergency off buttons are located in a spot that you will not hit inadvertently, but are easy to reach.

Warranty

Generally speaking, the higher quality treadmills will have longer warranties. I would recommend a warranty of at least 3 years for parts and one year for labor.

A number of manufacturers have started to offer life time warranties on their treadmills. This can be a very attractive feature if you plan to keep the machine for a long period of time. The machines with lifetime warranties, tend to be priced on the higher end. Make sure that you keep up all required cleaning and lubrication spelled out in the warranty. If you don't, the warranty could be voided.

Road Test

You should thoroughly check out each treadmill that you are considering. Before you start shopping, decide exactly what features you want, such as: programming and console features; heart rate controls; speed and incline; what you are using it for (fitness, weight loss, road racing, marathon training); frequency of use. During your test, watch for each of the following:

For the best service and selection, shop for a treadmill at a fitness or running specialty shop. This type of retailer will carry higher quality machines, their sales staff will be more knowledgeable and they will be able to provide superior service.

- **Noise** – Does the motor run quietly and smoothly? Does the incline motor run quietly?
- **Walk slowly** – Do the motor and belt operate smoothly at slow speeds? If the motor struggles at low speed, the treadmill may be engineered poorly.
- **Belt** – Does the belt operate smoothly at all speeds? Does it slip or slide off center? Is there excessive noise generated by the belt moving over the deck?
- **Size** – Do the belt and deck size accommodate your maximum stride with room to spare? Are you comfortable with the width of the belt?

- **Incline** – Does the treadmill incline smoothly? Does it feel stable when inclined?
- **Speed** – Does the top speed meet your training needs? If you plan to do your speed workouts on the treadmill you will need one that operates at higher speeds.
- **Controls** – Are the controls laid out in an easy to operate manner? Is the emergency off button located out of the way, but in an easy to reach area?
- **Heart rate monitor** – Does the treadmill have the heart rate controls that you want?
- **Smoothness** – Does the treadmill operate smoothly at all speeds? Do you notice any jerkiness or hesitation when accelerating or decelerating? Does the belt slip or hesitate?
- **Cushioning** – Is the level of cushioning appropriate for your training goals? Remember that if you are training for track or road racing you may not want a lot of cushioning. You will want to mimic actual competition conditions as much as possible. You will want less cushioning to condition your body to the actual conditions of running on asphalt, concrete or the artificial surfaces of tracks.

Try out a lot of treadmills before you buy. A quality treadmill is a major investment. A high end treadmill should last you many years, so be sure you are buying the one you are most comfortable with.

5

Treadmill Maintenance

An investment in a quality treadmill is a major financial commitment. In order to keep your treadmill operating efficiently and avoid expensive breakdowns you should follow a routine maintenance schedule. Keeping your treadmill clean and properly maintained 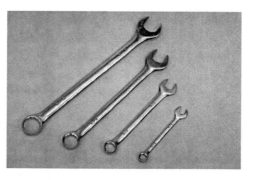 will extend the life of your belt, deck, rollers, motor and electronics. The following maintenance items should be followed on a consistent basis.

Treadmill Frame and Console

Wipe the treadmill frame and console with a damp cloth after every use. Clean all accumulated sweat and dirt from outside surfaces. It is best to use a cloth that is damp, but not wet. Check your owners manual for what type of cleaners to use and which to avoid. For most daily cleaning purposes, plain water will be the best choice.

Under and Around the Treadmill

The debris produced by the wearing of the belt and deck can soil carpet and other flooring under the treadmill. There are a number of mats available that are designed to be placed under the treadmill. These mats will help keep your flooring clean and also provide a stable surface for the treadmill.

Once a week, vacuum under and around the treadmill. You will notice a black dust or fine powder will accumulate behind and under the treadmill. This is caused by fine particles wearing off of the belt and deck. It is important to keep this debris and any other dust or dirt clear of the machine. This debris can be sucked into the motor and other moving parts of the treadmill and cause overheating and pre-mature wear. If this material is allowed to accumulate between the belt and deck, it will cause excessive friction. This friction will accelerate the wear on your deck and will place more stress on your rollers and motor.

Belt Alignment

It is important to keep the belt aligned in the center of the deck. A misaligned belt can cause excessive wear on one side of the rollers. It can also cause the belt to rub on the edge of the treadmill, which can decrease the life of the belt.

There are tracking adjustment bolts at the rear of the

machine on both sides. Make small adjustments. No more than 1/4 of a turn at a time. Follow your treadmill manufacturers directions on tracking and alignment adjustment. You should check the alignment each time you use the treadmill and adjust if necessary.

Belt Tension

The running belt will stretch slightly through use. The belt should never slip. If you feel the belt slipping, adjust it using the directions from the manufacturer. Be careful not to increase the tension too much. It should be tightened only enough to prevent slipping. If the belt is too tight, it will place excessive load on the rollers and on the motor.

To check the tension on your belt, bring the speed of your treadmill up to a slow walk. While walking slowly on the belt, bring your foot forcefully down and forward to try to make the belt slip. If you feel it slipping, increase the tension on the belt by 1/4 turn. Then check again. Repeat this if necessary, but remember not to make the belt too tight to avoid excessive wear.

Motor Compartment

The motor is located under the cowling at the front of the machine. The elevation motor is also located in that area. Once per month, you should disconnect the power cord and remove the cowling. Vacuum any dirt, dust, hair or debris from in and around the motor and other parts in the compartment. Be careful not to disturb wiring and electrical connections in this area. DO NOT REMOVE THE COWLING BEFORE UNPLUGGING THE TREADMILL.

Belt and Deck

Once a week, you should wipe down the belt surface with a damp cloth. You should also gently lift the edge of the belt and wipe between the belt and the deck.

It is important to keep the surface between the belt and the deck as low-friction as possible. High friction will cause high heat, which will cause premature deterioration of both the belt and the deck. Follow your manufacturers instructions concerning lubrication of the deck. Some treadmills have wax impregnated decks that require little maintenance. Others will require the application of a wax lubricant or a silicone lubricant.

Do not apply any lubricant before checking the manufacturers requirements. The wrong type of maintenance can void your warranty and cause expensive breakdowns. When applying a lubricant to your deck, you should use a minimum amount of the lubricant. If you apply too much, it can accumulate and cause excessive wear and tear.

6

Running on the Treadmill

Treadmill running should match, as closely as possible, free range running. Your running form should be the same. Your stride length and stride frequency should not change when you run on the treadmill. Your running mechanics  - foot plant, push off, posture, etc. should all be the same. If there were no differences between treadmill running and free range running, this would be simple and easy to accomplish.

Unfortunately, running on a treadmill is not the same as free range running. There are many differences. Some of these differences are positive and others are negative. The positive differences are good for everyone and need no adjustments. The negative differences can present a problem to some groups of runners. The first part of this chapter will be dedicated to overcoming these treadmill training problems.

Overcoming The Lack of Wind Resistance

The most obvious treadmill training problem is also the easiest to overcome. The lack of wind resistance and the assistance of the moving belt makes treadmill running easier than free range running. The fix for this problem is a matter of simply elevating the treadmill 1 percent. This will add enough of an incline to make your treadmill workout roughly equal to the same workout performed outside.

Most studies agree that adding a slight incline makes treadmill running nearly equal to outside running in terms of energy cost. But there has been a recent study that compared the energy cost of 100 meter sprinting on the track to the same workout on the treadmill. The results of that investigation showed that running on the track resulted in a whopping 36% increase in energy cost. Running the same workout on the treadmill was much easier. Studies using more typical, distance running speeds don't show that type of disparity between treadmill running and track running. But this does present questions on how the use of the treadmill effects high speed running. More studies are needed in this area before reliable conclusions can be drawn.

Maintaining Proper Running Form

As you know by now your training on the treadmill should match the training that you do outside on the road. Your running form should not change when you are training on the treadmill. That's sometimes easier said than done. The moving belt of the treadmill can create havoc with your running mechanics. The moving belt can cause some runners to lean too far forward at the waist in an attempt to "keep up" with the belt. Other runners may run with an extremely "bouncy" stride or may run with a very short and tight stride. You can avoid these form problems by focusing on your running mechanics.

All runners should concentrate on proper form when they run, whether they train on a treadmill or the road. This is especially important for new treadmill users. It is much better to perfect your form right away, rather than acquire bad running form habits that may be hard to break. Good running form is the same no matter where you train. Here are some runner form suggestions that will keep you running efficiently and injury free.

Posture

The most efficient running posture is one that is mostly upright and relaxed, with a slight, whole body, forward lean beginning at the ankles. You should not lean forward at the waist. Your chest should be pushed out and your shoulders back and relaxed. Avoid all tension in your upper body. Tension is a form wrecker.

Leaning too far forward at the waist will cause a stumbling, high impact motion that will slow you down and put excessive stress on your knees, hips and ankles. Leaning backward will cause you to run with too much vertical motion and will also stress your hips and back. Even the totally vertical posture that many running experts recommend has some built in stride inefficiencies. When running with a very vertical posture, you tend to reach out with both your legs and arms. This wastes energy and slows you down A slight, whole body, forward lean will enlist the help of gravity just enough to assist with directing your momentum smoothly forward.

Keep your hips pressed forward and your butt tucked in. Visualize standing face first against a wall. Press your hips forward so the front of your hips touch the wall. Running with your hips forward will help keep your motion going forward instead of up and down. It will also allow you to drive your knees efficiently forward.

Leaning Forward at the Waist

When you lean forward at the waist you're fighting gravity with every step. This will slow you down and place more stress on your joints. It also causes a shortening of your stride. Leaning forward at the waist will cause your hips to be pushed back. That will result in less knee drive, shorter stride length and more vertical motion. This is a common posture flaw among treadmill runners because of the tendency to try to push or keep up with the moving belt. Keep your butt tucked in and your body straight and relaxed with a slight forward lean. This whole body forward lean will allow you to use gravity rather than fight it.

Sitting in the Bucket

This is a common form flaw especially among beginning runners. The hips and butt are pushed out in the back resulting in a slight "sitting" position. "Sitting in the bucket" causes your feet to be in front of your body. You cannot use or maintain your forward momentum in this position and your stride becomes very vertical and bouncy. You waste a tremendous amount of energy with this form flaw. It is almost like running in place. Be sure you keep your hips pushed forward and your butt tucked in to avoid this error. Most of the action of your legs should take place behind your body. Concentrate on pushing off behind your body and pushing your hips forward.

Tense Upper Body

Tense muscles in your upper body means you are diverting valuable energy to muscles that do not need it. Keep your body relaxed and erect. Your jaw and face should be relaxed and pliable. Your shoulders and arms should be held in a loose and relaxed manner. Don't clench your fists. One good cue you can use is to imagine you're holding a butterfly in your hands. You want to hold onto it, but not crush it.

Stride Mechanics

The two components of running speed are stride length and stride rate. Stride length must be maximized in order to run your best, but you must accomplish this without over-striding. You must find the stride length that works best for you. Many top runners actually run with a shorter, quicker stride. But the important thing to remember is that they are running with the maximum stride length that works best for them. As a treadmill runner, you must pay especially close attention to maintaining your stride length, because the moving belt of the machine can easily cause you to over or under stride.

So how do you find our ideal stride length? You will fall into your best stride if you follow some stride key points. There are three components to running stride - Push off, flight and support.

Push Off

The push off is the portion of the stride when you drive off your rear foot. Most of the force generated from the push off comes from ankle joint extension and hip extension. Your ankle joint is extending when you are pushing the front of your foot down.

Push off with your rear foot and drive your lead knee forward. Push your hips forward, not your head and shoulders. Where your hips lead, your body will follow. This will keep all of the force you are generating, moving forward. If you push your head and shoulders forward, you will develop a forward lean at the waist.

Your push off leg should not be totally straight at the end of the push off. Keep the push off leg soft and slightly bent. This will help keep your body low to the ground and will maintain a forward direction to the force you are producing. A straight push off leg will result in a more up and down motion, which wastes energy and slows you down.

During the push off, the knee of your forward or swing leg should be driven forward. Don't try to lift your knee high. Concentrate on driving your knee forward. Your knee will automatically be driven higher as your speed increases. Let this happen naturally. Do not try to artificially drive your knee higher. Pick your feet up quickly. This will give you a light, quick running motion and you will waste less time on the running belt.

It is this combination of a push off, quick feet and a strong forward knee drive that will increase your stride length.

Your lower (calf) portion of your swing leg should fold up under your thigh. Think of your leg as a series of "levers". With your lower leg flexed or folded under your thigh, your leg becomes a shorter lever and will move much more efficiently. Imagine if your leg did not bend at the knee, and you tried to run. It would become very difficult to move the long lever of a straight leg with any efficiency.

Flight

During the flight phase, your body is totally in the air, with no support. At this point the lower leg and foot of your swing leg should begin to straighten and drop towards the ground so that at touch down your foot is directly under your center of gravity. Allow your forward momentum to "center" your body over your forward foot. If you attempt to reach out too far with that forward foot, you will land heavily on your heel, initiating a "braking" effect, which is overstriding.

It is at this point that both over striding and under striding can occur. As mentioned above, if you reach out too far in front of your body with the forward foot or do not allow the forward momentum of your body to "center" your body over your center of gravity, you will over stride and are slowing yourself down. If you drop your forward foot too quickly you will have a short, choppy stride and will not generate much speed. Just allow all of your forward momentum to remain in motion. Do not allow an overstride or understride to interrupt this valuable momentum.

Support

The support phase begins when your foot touches down and your leg is flexed. At this point your muscles are preparing for the next push off of the other leg. The touch down should be either flat footed or slightly on the ball of the foot, with the heel touching down just after the ball of the foot. If the heel strikes first, some over striding is present. Running with a slight whole body forward lean will encourage this flat footed support phase.

The most common form flaw is over striding. Always try to avoid reaching out in front of your body and landing on your heel. Your foot strike should be mostly flat footed or ball of your foot first, directly under your center of gravity.

Upon touchdown, the foot will flex slightly. This action will slightly stretch the powerful Achilles tendon just above the heel. This action "loads" the Achilles and the calf muscles with energy in preparation for another powerful push off. When running on the treadmill you should pay very close attention to this phase. Treadmill runners show an increase in the amount of time spent in the support phase. Longer time on the ground will result in a less efficient running stride and a decrease in running performance. Concentrate on being light on your feet with a quick and powerful push off. Try to forget you are on a treadmill and visualize moving smoothly forward.

Run Sneaky

Your stride should be light, quick and quiet. Try to run like you are sneaking up on someone. Your feet should be making as little noise as possible. A quiet stride means that you are running efficiently and powerfully. As I mentioned earlier in this chapter, the best way to achieve a quick, quiet and sneaky stride is to pick your feet up quickly. A heavy and slow stride results when you spend too much time with your feet on the ground or running belt in the support phase.

Arm Action

Arm action is basically for balance and coordination. Keep your arms loose and relaxed. Do not waste energy by clenching your fists or tightening muscles in your arms and shoulders. Let your shoulders swing freely. Any tension in your upper body can translate to tension throughout your body.

Most top runners keep their arms bent approximately 90 degrees at the elbows. During the arm swing, most of the movement is behind the body. Try not to let your hands travel above your chest. Don't cross your arms in front of your body. A common arm action flaw is reaching out in front of your body. This wastes energy and can result in a number of problems, including over striding. Concentrate on driving your elbows back and keeping your arm action compact. You should feel almost as if you are trying to elbow the runner behind you.

Beating Psychological Hurdles

Boredom

The most common and most obvious psychological problem associated with treadmill running is boredom. Treadmill running can be very tedious. You do not have scenery moving by or changing terrain to keep you occupied. There are no other runners, unless you are running in a gym. There is no traffic and no other people around. All you have to keep you occupied is how tired you are getting and how much you want to stop. In order to avoid stopping due to sheer boredom, you need to add some diversion to keep your mind active.

Your treadmill training sessions provide a good opportunity for some guilt free television time. The television will also provide some entertainment to help you avoid the boredom problem.

Most treadmill runners will either watch television or listen to music while they are running. A good movie will make the time fly by. There are some runners that get too distracted by the television and prefer to listen to music. You should use whatever method you prefer and works best for you. Your treadmill workout should be enjoyable, so do whatever you need to do in order to make it fun.

External entertainment, such as television or music will help keep your boredom level down. You can also make changes to your training program that will keep you interested and motivated. One of the greatest advantages to treadmill running, is the ability to do absolutely any type of workout, including hill training. Even if you live in a flat area, you can do hill work on your treadmill. You can design an unlimited number of workouts that combine anything from short fast repeats to long slow distance. Keep changing your workouts. If you do the same workout every day, you will get bored quickly. In addition to avoiding boredom, doing a variety of workouts will get you in better condition, and if you race, it will improve your race performance.

You can also play games on the treadmill. Try to beat your previous PR (personal record). Do 5K or 10K races on your treadmill. Run while watching a racing movie or a marathon. I tape a lot of televised marathons. One game I play is doing my long runs while watching a marathon. I imagine I am out there running with the competitors. Use your imagination. Try not to dwell on the boredom. Learn to imagine and play games in your head and you will find that treadmill running can be just as enjoyable as outside running.

The objective of treadmill training is to make the workout as similar to free range running as possible and also as enjoyable as possible. This is easily done with just a little practice, imagination and the following tips.

Staying Motivated

Another challenge of treadmill training is staying motivated. Using a treadmill in an empty room provides very little in the way of motivation. Running while looking at a blank wall should probably be considered a form of torture. The treadmill is not an instrument of torture. It is a valuable training tool and can be a very enjoyable way to run. With just a few adjustments to your environment and your training habits, you can stay motivated for workout after workout.

Environment

If you have your own treadmill, try to place it in a position in which you have a view from a window. You may not be moving, but something outside is. You can see changing weather conditions, animals, children, cars, anything to engage your mind even a little bit.

If you are using a treadmill in a gym, there will probably be a window nearby. At the very least you will have other members of your club and other machines nearby to keep your attention. If you have a home gym, make your environment as pleasant as possible. Keep it clean and clutter free. Paint it a color that you like. Install a water cooler for easy access to cold water. Do anything you can to make your workout area a place that you enjoy.

Entertainment

Almost all experienced treadmill runners do one of two things. They either watch television or listen to music while they run. Your treadmill workout is, in fact, a very good time to enjoy some guilt free television. When else can you watch TV and not feel like you should be doing something more productive? Some walkers read while they exercise. This is not suggested for runners for two reasons.

- It is very difficult to read while you are running. There is simply too much movement to make out the words clearly.
- When you are running, it is important to focus on your form, mechanics, stride, breathing, etc. You can watch the boob tube and listen to music without having to concentrate on them. Reading requires concentration that should be reserved for your training run.

Watching television is an ideal method of adding entertainment to your workout area. Most runners can watch television without losing the focus and concentration that is sometimes required when training. Any television will work, but of course a larger set will make it easier to see while running. Place your television in front of your treadmill. It should be close enough to see without squinting, but far enough away so that it does not present a hazard. Don't forget that you may be sweating heavily during your workout. If the TV is too close, some of your sweat could fly onto the set. A VCR or DVD player will increase your entertainment options. A two hour movie is just about right for many of your long runs. Make sure your television is located in a

Use Velcro strips to attached remote controls, and other items that you may need, to your treadmill frame. They will always be within easy reach.

stable position. Running on the treadmill can cause some bouncing of the floor. If the television is placed on top of an unstable television stand, the bouncing of the floor could possibly cause the stand to topple.

If you have the ability to connect external speakers to your television, you may want to consider doing so. Even with the quietest treadmills, it is sometimes hard to hear the small television speakers when you are running. Try to mount the speakers above and just in front of the treadmill. This position will give you the best acoustical advantage. If there are other family members living in your home, they will appreciate the lower speaker volume.

Using Feedback Data

Almost all motorized treadmills will display your total calories burned, total miles, current speed and total time. Some will also give you calories per hour, average speed, current pace, average pace and heart rate data.

Using the abundance of data that is available can be both entertaining and motivating. You can scan through the data and see your progress in the workout. You could also set goals for average pace, calories burned, distance or time.

For many runners, the use of the console feedback functions is a motivational tool, but for some, watching the miles and minutes tick by on the console only adds to the tedium and makes the workout seem longer. A bit like watching paint dry. Some of these runners will drape their workout towel over the display so they cannot see it. I would discourage this practice, because the towel can fall off the console onto the moving belt and trip you as you are running.

Workout Variety

Perhaps the greatest advantage to treadmill training is the vast, nearly unlimited number of possible workouts you can do. Take advantage of this. Doing the same work-outs day after day will get very tedious. It is not only bor-ing, but your body will "learn" those workouts and you will not increase your fitness as quickly as you could be. Mix up your workouts. There are a number of different work-outs for each type of training run in the workouts chapter of this book. Try them all and then make up some of your own. Make your workouts challenging. Variety and chal-lenge will keep you interested and motivated.

Play Games

Play games to defeat boredom, using the feedback data. Run some practice 5K or 10K races. Try to beat your previ-ous personal records for each workout. Do some hill work-outs and try to beat your hill distance record. Use your imagination and keep your mind active. Have fun with your workout. Make it a play time. There is nothing wrong with playing and having fun. As many of us get older we begin to take everything very seriously and either do not make time

for play or feel that play is only for children. The next time you feel bored with your workout, think back on when you were a child. You were never bored. You made a game out of everything. You can still do the same thing. Make up imaginary competitors in your mind. Race these phantom runners when you are on the treadmill. Imagine yourself breaking away from the pack and winning the Boston Marathon. Pretend you are running over soft pine needles through a quiet forest trail. Just have fun and you will not be bored.

Other Psychological Challenges

The other primary psychological problems - lack of visual cues, perception of limited room, and lack of confidence must be overcome with practice and experience. The disorientation associated with the lack of moving scenery should not be a problem after the first week or two of treadmill running. Most treadmill users adapt even faster than that.

The perception of limited room and lack of confidence will be overcome with experience. Once you do a few workouts and discover that you will not step off the machine, you will gain confidence. The lack of confidence in the training benefits may take a bit longer. Your trust in the training will grow as you discover your level of exertion when training. One good way to increase your confidence is to go to the track and do a speed workout. Then go home an hop on your treadmill and do the same workout. You will find that your workout on the treadmill will feel as hard if not harder than your track workout.

Meeting the Law of Specificity

This one you cannot overcome without doing some outside running. You are not training to race on a treadmill. In order to meet this very important law of training, you should do some training that matches that of your goal race. If you are training for road racing, you should do some training on the road. If your goal race is a trail run, you should do some of your training runs on the trail. If you race on the track, some track training is necessary.

How much specific training is necessary? That depends upon your goals and your goal race distance. If you simply want to finish your race and are not concerned with finishing time, you can do most, if not all, of your runs on the treadmill. If race performance is important to you, more of your runs should be done outside. Race distance also dictates how much specific training should be done. Recent studies have suggested that during slower running speeds there is little difference between treadmill training and free range running. As running speed increases, the difference between the two methods of training also increases. So, since shorter race distance means faster running speed - shorter race distances also require more outside running. There will be specific recommendations concerning outside running in the individual training programs.

Overcoming Running Surface Differences

This is another difficult problem to overcome. The smooth and even surface of the treadmill cannot be made rough and uneven. The main negative result of this is the lack of propreoceptive training.

Learning and Maintaining Proprioception

Proprioception is an important skill when running on the treadmill. Proprioception is basically intuitively feeling and knowing the position and motion of your body, feet, legs, arms, etc. at all times. It is being aware of all of the different actions of your running stride. This is something that, to a limited extent, you do naturally. But to maximize your level of awareness, practice consciously being aware of your position on the belt, the amount of forward lean, the position of your hips, the angle of your feet and all stages of your running stride.

When running outside, you encounter all types of uneven and unstable running surfaces. This type of surface will force your neuromuscular system to become more proprioceptive because it must make split second adjustments in order to keep your body stable and moving in the right direction. The flat and even surface of the treadmill takes away this valuable skill. So, if you do most or all of your workouts on the treadmill, you should practice proprioception at all times. You can also use a wobble board. A wobble board is just what it sounds like. It is a board with a half sphere on the bottom of it. It "wobbles" when you step or stand on it. Use of this type of board will help build and maintain those proprioceptive skills.

Proprioception is important in all running activities, but even more so when running on the treadmill. Runners tend to allow the action of the belt and the lack of wind resistance to change their stride to a more upright, bouncy form with a shorter, less powerful stride. Being more aware of your running mechanics will make it easier to transfer your normal stride to the treadmill.

Adapting to Treadmill Running

The first difference in treadmill training that must be overcome is mounting and dismounting the treadmill. A moving treadmill belt is traveling at between 1 and 12 miles per hour. If you are careless in getting on or off the machine, you could find yourself airborne instead of running.

The proper way to mount a treadmill is to stand on the machine with the belt stopped and your feet placed firmly on the frame on each side of the belt. Start the belt at its slowest setting and carefully step onto the belt, one foot at a time. Once you are on the moving belt and walking steadily, gradually increase the speed of the belt to your desired speed. To dismount, slow the belt gradually to a stop and then step off. Some treadmills have an emergency off switch. If you press this switch, the treadmill will slow and stop very quickly. This can throw you off balance. For this reason, when stopping the treadmill, you should gradually decrease the speed using the speed controls and then stop it using the normal off switch. The emergency off switch should be reserved for its intended emergency use. There are also some treadmills that use a safety key. There is a cord on this key that is intended to be wrapped around your body with the key inserted into the treadmill. The treadmill will not operate without this key. The idea is that if you are thrown off the treadmill, your body will pull the key out and shut down the machine. If you use this system, be sure there is enough slack in the cord. If the cord is too tight, your normal movement on the machine could cause the key to be pulled out and shut down the treadmill. This could take you by surprise and knock you off balance.

A lot of experienced treadmill runners will mount and dismount the treadmill with the belt moving at running speed. I would discourage this practice for most users for the obvious safety reasons.

As we discussed earlier, running form and mechanics on a treadmill should be no different than free range running. But, for the first few sessions, this will probably not be the case. Your first steps on a treadmill will probably feel awkward and unsteady. This will not last long. Most runners adapt very well to treadmill running within the first session or two. It takes some practice, but any runner will be able to duplicate and even improve their stride on the treadmill.

When you first start running on a treadmill, it will feel different and probably a bit disconcerting. The first few times you step off the treadmill after a workout, you may feel slightly dizzy and disoriented. This is the psychological effect caused by the lack of visual cues indicating movement. You will adapt to this quickly and it should not be a chronic problem. Be careful if you do feel dizzy or disoriented. Step off the treadmill carefully and hold on to something solid to steady yourself until the feeling passes.

Run slowly for your first few treadmill workouts and concentrate on maintaining your normal stride. Focus on keeping a strong push off with your back foot and a forceful forward knee drive with your forward leg. There is a strong tendency for beginning treadmill runners to shorten their stride and spend more time with their feet on the belt.

Try to keep your stride free and loose with a lot of push off. You will want keep your float (the portion of your stride in which you are in the air) at its maximum. As you become more comfortable on the machine, go ahead and gradually increase your speed. Start to vary your workouts. You will soon be able to do all of your various training runs with no discomfort.

Run on the center of the belt. Do not run towards the

back or the front of the machine. If you run too far forward on the belt, you may find yourself striking the cowling on the front of the machine. If you run too far towards the back of the belt, you risk stepping off the back of the treadmill.

One bad habit that you want to avoid is hanging onto the handles or frame of the treadmill while you run. However, as you are adapting to running on a moving belt, do not hesitate to grab the handles to steady yourself. If you feel like you are losing your balance or are in danger of falling off the machine, grab the handles until your balance is recovered.

Training Methods

There are three major methods of training. Heart rate training, recent race times and training by your rate of perceived exertion. Each has advantages in certain situations. Here are the basics of each type of training and some recommendations.

Heart rate training

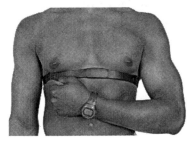

Training by heart rate has become very popular over the past several years. This is a very common method of treadmill training because many treadmills have built in heart rate monitors. There are even some upper end treadmills that will automatically adjust speed and incline to keep you within your desired exercise heart rate. When training by heart rate, you wear a belt around your lower chest that has a sensor built into it. The sensor sends heart rate data to a receiver that you either wear on your wrist or that is built into the treadmill.

Heart rate training is based upon two heart rates - your maximum heart rate and your target heart rate. Your maximum heart rate is the highest rate at which your heart will beat. This can be determined by a monitored treadmill test or can be estimated with the formula of 220 minus your age. If you are 40 years old, your estimated maximum heart rate would be 220 - 40 = 180 beat per minute.

You can also determine your maximal heart rate on the treadmill or track. Warm up thoroughly with some easy running and some short sprints. You should be warmed up enough to engage in highly intense running. Now run 1/2 mile as fast as you can, while wearing a heart rate monitor. Check your heart rate in the last 30 seconds of your 1/2 mile run. If you ran this test as hard as you can, this should be your maximal heart rate. If your treadmill does not go fast enough for you to run your hardest, you will have to do this test on the track.

Your target heart rate is a range of rates that your training program will specify for each workout. You will run at a pace that elicits the desired heart rate. You will either slow down or speed up in order to keep your heart rate at the desired level. The theory is that each of the different types of workouts - easy runs, speed workouts, lactate threshold runs, hill workouts; are best performed at a specific heart rate level.

Target heart rate is calculated using one of several formulas. The two most commonly used are the percentage of maximal heart rate and the Karvonen formula.

Percentage of Maximal Heart Rate

This formula is maximum heart rate x desired training percentage x 1.15. For example, our 40 year old athlete will have an estimated maximum heart rate of 180 beats per minute. If this athlete wanted to run at a pace that results in a heart rate of 70% of maximum heart rate, the formula would be as follows:

180 x 70% = 126   126 x 1.15 = 145 beats per minute.

In this example, the target heart rate for your training run would be 145 beats per minute. The heart rate is multiplied by 1.15 because recent research has shown that a straight percentage of the maximal heart rate is too conservative for most runners.

Your target heart rate will vary according to your fitness level and what type of workout you are doing. It may vary from 50% of your maximum heart rate to 95%.

Karvonen Formula

The Karvonen formula is similar to the percentage of maximal heart rate. The difference is that the Karvonen formula incorporates the resting heart rate. Resting heart rate is the rate that your heart beats when at rest. It is best measured just before getting out of bed. Measure you pulse at your wrist or neck. Count the number of beats in 10 seconds and multiply by 6. This will give you the beats per minute.

The Karvonen formula is maximum heart rate - resting heart rate x desired intensity + resting heart rate. Using the same 40 year old, desiring an intensity of 70% of maximum heart rate, with a maximum heart rate of 180 bpm and a resting heart rate of 80 beats per minute, the formula would be as follows:

$$180 - 80 = 100 \quad 100 \times 70\% = 70 \quad 70 + 80 = 150 \text{ beats}$$
per minute

The physiological difference between the two methods is heart rate reserve. The Karvonen formula factors in this reserve which is basically the reserve of the heart to increase its output. Both formulas are commonly used. Of the two, the Karvonen formula is usually the most accurate.

Advantages and Disadvantages

One of the most common errors committed by beginning runners is running too hard on easy run days. Heart rate training offers the advantage of not letting you run harder than you should be on your easy days. You can set the monitor to alert you if your heart rate goes too high.

The main disadvantage of heart rate training is a lack of accuracy. Estimated maximum heart rates are based on very generalized statistics that have a built in variation of up to 19 beats per minute. This means that if you are exercising at 70% of your maximum heart rate, you may be working out at up to 17 beats per minute too fast or too slow. In addition, all athletes are different. There are many people who can exercise comfortably at up to 36 beats faster than the recommended maximum and there are those who must keep their heart rate well below the recommended maximum. If these runners were to blindly follow the recommended heart rates, they would either be exercising at too high or too low an intensity level.

Your training heart rate will also vary according to both external and internal factors. High heat conditions, dehydration, fatigue, stress, illness and medications can all cause your heart rate to increase or decrease, which will affect the accuracy of heart rate training.

During exercise, your heart rate tends to increase in the last half of workouts or races, even if you do not increase your intensity, due to a condition known as cardiac drift. If you follow the suggestions for heart rate training, you will decrease the intensity of your exercise in order to get your heart rate back down to the recommended level, but in the case of cardiac drift, you will actually be working a too low a level.

The appropriate training heart rate will vary according to the specific training zones. Here are training heart rate ranges for each type of training run.

- Endurance - 70% to 80%
- Speed Endurance - 80% to 90%
- Speed - 90% to 95%
- Speed/Strength - 95% to 100%

Training by Current Race Times

You can use your current 5K or 10K race times to calculate an appropriate training pace. If you complete your 5K races at the maximum intensity that you can maintain, you are running at about 5% over your anaerobic or lactate threshold, which is the pace at which you begin to build up more lactic acid in your blood than your muscles can process.. In a 10K race you are running about 2.5% over your anaerobic threshold pace. Using your race pace as a guideline, you can calculate a relatively accurate training pace for each type of workout that you do.

If you only run 5K races and need to estimate your 10K race pace simply add 20 seconds per mile to your 5K pace. That will give you a close estimate.

The advantage to this type of training is that it is customized to each individual, instead of relying upon general statistical data. Your training pace will also adjust itself as you gain or lose fitness.

The disadvantage of race time training is that you must have completed and consistently compete in races. You must also compete at a maximum intensity in the races. If you are new to running or have not completed at least 5 races at your best intensity, this may not be an accurate method. You will have to compete in races on a consistent basis in order to get updated feedback on your race times. As your race times improve, you will increase your training pace. If your race performance decreases, you will also decrease the pace of your training runs.

Training By Rate of Perceived Exertion

Listening to your body has a lot of advantages. There are more variables involved in how fast you should run than just heart rate. Your stress level, physical health, emotional health, temperature, humidity, the time of day, the last time you ate and what you ate, all contribute to the intensity at which you should run. If you listen to your body, it will tell you all of these things.

The rate of perceived exertion (RPE), also know as the Borg scale, was developed by Swedish physiologist G.A.V. Borg. This scale rates exercise intensity from 6 to 20 depending upon how the athlete feels or perceives his or her effort. The scale is as follows:

Rating of Perceived Exertion Levels

- 6   Minimal
- 7   Very,very light
- 8   Very,very light +
- 9   Very light
- 10   Very light +
- 11   Fairly light
- 12   Comfortable
- 13   Somewhat hard
- 14   Somewhat hard +
- 15   Hard
- 16   Hard +
- 17   Very hard
- 18   Very hard +
- 19   Very,very hard
- 20   Maximal

You can get an approximate heart rate level for each rating by simply adding a zero to each rating. For example a rating of 12 will result in an approximate heart rate of 120 beats per minute.

Your RPE will vary depending upon the factors discussed earlier. That is the major benefit of this type of training. If your body is strong and rested, you will feel strong and your pace will feel easier. When your body is in this condition, you are able to train harder and the RPE will support this. If you feel tired and sluggish, it is because your body needs a break. In this condition, your pace will feel harder. Again, this will show up in your RPE and you will train at the proper level for that day.

Suggestions

In the past several years, heart rate training and training in the "Zone" have been the most popular methods of training. Many runners, especially beginners, have become preoccupied with their heart rate and will blindly follow it no matter how they are feeling. Heart rate formulas are all based on statistics that have built in variations. Your MHR (maximum heart rate) has a variation of up to plus or minus 19 beats per minute. There is another built in variation of plus or minus 17 beats per minute when you are exercising at 70% of your MHR, which is the "zone" heart rate that has become so popular. That means you could be exercising at up to 30 beats per minute faster or slower than you should be. That is a large potential error.

If you participate in local races your most recent race pace is the most accurate way to determine your training pace. If you don't know your race pace, perceived exertion is the most reliable alternative.

So what is the best training method? I believe that if you are a competitive athlete that consistently competes in races, race pace training is a good way to go. This will keep your training pace constantly adjusted to the pace that will give you the greatest improvement in race times. If you are a beginner or are running mostly for pleasure and fitness gains, the rate of perceived exertion is the way to go. This will allow you to customize a training plan with the least amount of calculation or time involved. It will be the most accurate gauge of intensity because it will take into consideration, the current health and strength of your body.

Heart rate training can be a good training tool as long as you understand its limitations and its potential lack of accuracy. The convenience of the built in heart rate monitoring in treadmills makes this method very attractive for many runners.

Keeping Cool

One primary difference between treadmill and free range running, is the self generated wind that keeps you cool when you run outside. If you are running at 8 MPH, you are, in effect, generating an 8 MPH wind in your face. That wind performs a great service in evaporating your sweat and keeping you cool. When you run on the treadmill, you are running in place and are not generating that wind. So, you must turn to other methods to keep yourself cool.

The easiest way to keep cool is to place a fan in front of your treadmill. When you start to get too hot, just turn on the fan. The breeze generated by the fan will do the same job as the wind you generate outside. A fan with a remote control is a very handy feature. It will allow you to control the direction and the speed of the fan from your treadmill.

Air conditioning and open windows will help keep you cool, but neither will help as much as a breeze directed at your body. A ceiling fan located over the treadmill is also a good way to keep cool, but again, a fan blowing a breeze at your body will make your treadmill workout more like running outside, and that is the goal of treadmill running.

Keep a stock of workout towels nearby. It will come in handy for wiping sweat off of both your body and the treadmill when you are done. I like to keep a stock of towels nearby along with a container to toss the used towels into for later laundering.

Staying Hydrated

Another great benefit of treadmill training, is that you will always have plenty of fluids nearby. No worries about bringing a sufficient amount of fluid with you. Running outside you either have to carry it with you or hide it in a nearby bush.

Be sure that you stay well hydrated when running on the treadmill. Just because you are not exercising in the sunlight, does not mean that you are not depleting your body of fluids. Your body is constantly using fluids to cool itself and water is a by product of the production of energy. Follow the same hydration habits that you follow when running outdoors.

Hydration recommendations have changed somewhat in recent years. Experts used to recommend drinking be-

fore you are thirsty and drinking at least 8 ounces every 15 minutes. The theory was that if you waited until you were thirsty to drink, you were already dehydrated and you would have a hard time "catching up" with your hydration needs. Those rec-

ommendations are starting to change due to some recent events involving excessive water consumption.

There have been a lot of recent incidents of hyponatremia, especially in marathon runners. Hyponatremia is a condition caused by drinking too much water and diluting the sodium concentration in your blood, which is a dangerous condition.

In order to reduce the chances of suffering from this serious ailment, the latest recommendations suggest drinking only when you are thirsty and consuming a sports drink containing sodium when running for more than one hour. This is probably a bit of an over-reaction. Hypona-tremia is rarely a concern for the vast majority of athletes and is never a problem with any runs or workouts of less than 90 minutes. The problem with this recommendation is that your thirst does lag behind you hydration level. If you wait until you are thirsty, you are already dehydrated. So, I would suggest continuing to drink every 15 minutes. If you are doing a run in excess of 1 hour, include that so-dium containing sports drink.

If you are exercising for less than one hour, there is little chance of developing hyponatremia. Drinking plain water will work fine, unless you are working out in a high heat environment. In that case, you should use a fluids replacement drink.

7

Training on the Treadmill

Acommon question I get from athletes I coach is, "how can I use the treadmill within my existing training program"? The answer to that question is very simple. You can do nearly any of your current workouts on the treadmill. One of the few exceptions is if you're doing some of your speed workouts at faster than the top speed of the treadmill. Many treadmills have a top speed of at least 10 m.p.h., which is a 6:00 mile. Some of the high end treadmills top out at 12 m.p.h., which is a 5:00 mile. You can find treadmills that go faster, but they start to get extremely expensive at that point.

A treadmill that does up to a 5:00 mile will be sufficient for all but the fastest runners. If you are one of the fortunate few that do your speed work at faster than 5:00 per mile, you will have to do at least some of your speed training at the track.

Every category of runner from a beginner to an elite marathon runner, can do a few, a lot or even all of their training runs on the treadmill and achieve satisfactory results.

Beginning Runners

The treadmill is an ideal training tool for beginning runners. Most beginners begin with a walking or a walk/run program. The treadmill makes it very easy to make the transition from walking to running. Just increase the speed slightly for a brief period of time before slowing back down to a walk.

The convenience of the treadmill will help a beginning runner stick to their program. It eliminates all excuses for not working out. If you don't feel like doing your workout try just putting on your running shoes. Just that simple act of getting ready to run can motivate you to get your workout in.

The convenience of a treadmill provides a huge motivational advantage for beginning runners. Your treadmill is available at any time of the day. You do not have to worry about weather, darkness or safety. It removes all excuses for not doing your workout. You never have an excuse for not doing your workout. Beginning runners without a treadmill can come up with a long list of excuses for not doing their training run. Bad weather, darkness, air pollution, lack of time, work commitments, social commitments, etc. When you can just hop on your treadmill for 20 minutes, those excuses don't hold water anymore.

A beginning runner can do some or all of their workouts on the treadmill. A training program for beginners is designed to improve cardiovascular fitness, muscular strength, muscular endurance, connective tissue strength and mental toughness. All of these goals can be achieved by running on the treadmill.

The softer running surface makes treadmill running even more advantageous for beginners. It is very important for beginning runners to gradually improve the strength of their joints and connective tissues. If these tissues are subjected to more stress than they are conditioned for, physical breakdowns can occur. This is where most running injuries happen and beginners are especially susceptible. The constant pounding of running on concrete or asphalt puts much more stress on the joints than running on the softer surface of the treadmill does. Running on the more cushioned treadmill surface allows a new runner's muscles and joints to adapt more gradually to this new physical stress that they are being subjected to.

Treadmills are also more forgiving to the stride of a freshman runner. A beginning runner has usually not yet developed their stride to the point that it is smooth and efficient. The bouncy, up and down running stride of a beginner also puts more stress on the joints and tendons, which the softer treadmill surface will help smooth out.

I would suggest that beginners do all poor weather workouts on the treadmill. A beginner has not yet developed their proprioceptive abilities and balance that is necessary to run safely on uneven or slippery surfaces. Running outside in bad weather can also cause any runner to cut their workout short or skip it altogether. If I look outside and see blowing snow, I start looking for excuses not to go out and run in the bad weather. With the treadmill in easy reach, I would not even consider missing my workout in bad weather. I just hop on and run. The quality of your run will also suffer when running in bad weather, because of the uncertain footing and uncomfortable conditions. It is much better to run inside on the treadmill and get a good workout than to run outside in bad weather and get a poor workout.

For safety reasons, all nighttime workouts should also be done on the treadmill. Running in the dark presents several hazards, including: traffic, road obstacles and criminal activity. These are all easily avoided by running on the treadmill.

Any fair weather, daylight runs can be done outside. But do not feel as if you have to run outside. In more advanced training programs, it is advisable to do some outside running. But, as a beginner, feel free to do all of your workouts on the treadmill. Your fitness gains will be equal or superior to what you would achieve by running outside.

Recreational and Fitness Runners

For the purposes of this book, a recreational or fitness runner is considered someone who has been running consistently for at least 3 months. The goals of a recreational/fitness runner may include weight loss, fitness and health gains, stress reduction, lifestyle change or just plain old fun. This type of runner is usually not interested in racing, performance gains or pace.

Weight Loss

If you want to increase the rate of your calorie burn without increasing your pace, try increasing the incline of the treadmill. Each 1 percent increase in elevation will raise the rate of calorie burn by approximately 4% to 15% depending upon your weight, pace and amount of incline.

Just as with a beginner, a runner training to lose weight can do any or all of their workouts on the treadmill. To meet the goal of weight loss, calorie burn is the primary objective. It does not matter whether the calorie is burned on the treadmill or outside. A calorie burned is a calorie burned.

The console of the treadmill provides valuable feedback for weight loss users. The runner will be able to monitor total calories burned and calories per hour. This kind of information can be critical to the success of a weight loss program.

If weight loss is your long-term goal, consider setting a specific number of calories burned as your workout goal. Weight loss is a function of calories in versus calories out. Once you know how many calories you are burning during exercise, you can add in the calories burned by your daily activities and basal metabolic rate (BMR). Your BMR is the number of calories that you expend just by living and breathing. You can estimate your BMR using the following calculations:

• Men - Multiply your weight by 10 and add twice your weight to this value.
• Women - Multiply your weight by 10 and add your weight to this value.

Adding the approximate calories burned through your daily activities will allow you to calculate roughly how many total calories you should be eating in order to maintain the negative calorie balance required for weight loss.

Runners with the goal of weight loss enjoy the same motivational advantages as beginning runners. The treadmill removes all excuses for not exercising.

Many individuals that are exercising for weight loss, are limited to walking. Use the elevation features of your treadmill to increase the rate of calorie burn. Increasing the elevation has a similar calorie burning effect as increasing pace. The higher the elevation, the more calories per hour you are burning.

Fitness, Health, Stress Reduction & Lifestyle Change

Many individuals run in order to change their formally sedentary lifestyle, increase their fitness levels, improve their health and reduce the stress in their life.

Most runners of this type typically run 3 to 5 times per week. They usually run at the same pace and on the same routes. All of these types of runs can be done on the treadmill with no decrease in benefits.

Running on the treadmill can actually increase the returns by providing some variety in terrain and speed. Hills can be easily added in by elevating the treadmill. Speed can be increased for short periods. The addition of some hill running and short increases in speed will improve fitness levels more and faster than mono-speed running on level terrain outside.

Competitive Runners

A competitive runner is one who trains in order to improve their racing performance and speed. They do not necessarily have to compete for top positions, but they want to run at the best pace that they can.

The treadmill is a valuable tool for a competitive runner, but, in most cases better results will be achieved by including some free-range running. There have been contradictory results obtained from the limited number of studies concerning the efficiency of treadmill running. Most of the studies have shown that there is very little difference in the physiological response of treadmill training versus free range training. Fitness gains are nearly identical. But, there have been a couple of studies that have shown that treadmill running has less of an energy cost and is therefore a less efficient method of training. Until conclusive evidence is presented, we must use what data is available and what our experiences tell us. My personal experience in both my coaching career and my own training tells me that the majority of studies are correct. The physiological gains are very similar at most distance running speeds. But if you want to run your best, your training should mimic your goal event as closely as possible. This means doing at least some of your workouts on the road, track or trail.

The rule of specificity states that training should match the goal as closely as possible. The treadmill will equal free range workouts for most purposes, but is very different than free range running. The most important differences between treadmill and free range running are:

- Lack of wind resistance on the treadmill. When running outside the density of the air adds some extra resistance that you must overcome. Since you are not moving through the air when running on the treadmill, that extra resistance is not present.
- The moving belt does part of the work when running on the treadmill. You are keeping pace with a moving surface rather than forcefully propelling yourself over the ground. If you do not focus on maintaining your stride mechanics, treadmill running can cause minor stride inefficiencies that could carry over into your outside running.
- The treadmill has a softer, more forgiving surface than the asphalt and concrete surfaces most commonly encountered in road racing. While this softer surface is great for decreasing the impact of running and reducing the chances of injury, it does not prepare you adequately for the more firm surfaces you will be running on while road racing.
- No environmental challenges on the treadmill. When you race outside you will run into all types of weather conditions. Heat, cold, rain, snow and wind can all become factors during a race. The treadmill removes these factors.
- Psychological differences. If you believe that you are not getting a good workout on the treadmill, it can affect the quality of your workout and your subsequent free range efforts.

As you know by now, the lack of wind resistance is a major difference between treadmill running and outside running. This becomes more important as you run faster. When walking or running very slowly, there is not much of an effect from wind resistance. However, as you pick up your pace, more resistance is generated. The physiological effect of the lack of wind resistance and the moving belt can be adequately offset by elevating the treadmill 1 or 2 percent. When running between 5 and 9 MPH, 1 percent elevation is adequate. When running faster than 9 MPH, elevate the treadmill 1.5% or 2% to compensate for the additional resistance of faster running.

The difference between the softer surface of the treadmill and the firmer roads cannot be completely overcome. There are treadmills available that have a fairly firm deck. Some are made of wood which give a very firm ride. But even with the firmer deck, there is some flexibility in the frame and additional cushioning in the suspension system that makes the treadmill workout a more cushioned run.

For many running goals, the softer surface of a treadmill is an advantage. It decreases the stress on the joints and helps avoid injuries. But a competitive road runner must be conditioned to run on concrete, asphalt, dirt, grass and uneven surfaces. These surfaces are much harder and less forgiving than the most firm treadmill. If all of your training runs are done on the softer surface, when you run outside on harder or more uneven surfaces you could encounter joint pain, muscle pain, premature fatigue and possible injury.

The effects of the moving belt will become more pronounced as your running speed increases. Research has shown that experienced runners will run with similar stride length during slow running on both the treadmill and outside. But, as running speed increases, experienced runners tend to increase their stride length past their most efficient level. Beginning runners have the opposite problem. They tend to run with a stride length that is too short when doing fast treadmill running. So pay close attention to your mechanics when doing fast training runs on the treadmill.

Environmental conditions, such as heat, cold, wind, rain, snow and ice, obviously cannot be duplicated on the treadmill. It is usually best to avoid these conditions. I would suggest that even competitive runners avoid running outside on ice or snow due to the chance of injury, changes in running stride when running on ice or snow and the nearly unavoidable decrease in the quality of the workout. Some runners actually enjoy running in the rain.

I am not one of them. I am a card carrying member of the poor weather wimp club. So, I am on the treadmill any time I do not like the conditions outside. But, other than periods of snow, ice, extreme heat, extreme cold, high pollution or high winds, running outside in less than ideal conditions is usually not hazardous. So if you enjoy it - go for it.

The decision of whether or not to run on the treadmill during poor weather conditions will depend upon your specific goal race. If you are training for a marathon that will be held in hot weather, you should do some of your training runs, including some long runs, outside in the heat. Always remember the rule of specificity. If your goal race will be hot, you must train in some heat. Just make sure you stay hydrated and be careful of dehydration, heat exhaustion and heat stroke.

The same reasoning applies to cold weather running. If your goal race is held during cold weather, you will be better prepared if you do some of your training runs in cold weather.

The psychological problem of lack of confidence in the quality of treadmill training is one that is easily overcome, but it could take some time. Some runners do not lose any confidence when treadmill training, while others do not trust the quality of treadmill training. It is usually experienced runners that have not used a treadmill for competitive training that have problems with trust. The only way for them to overcome this is to do some consistent training on the treadmill and see for themselves that their performance does not deteriorate and in many cases actually improves.

The bottom line is this: If you are a competitive runner and want to maximize your race performance, you should do some of your training runs outside. There is no oth-

Do you lack confidence in the ability of your treadmill to give you a quality workout? Give it a test. Go to the track and do a speed workout that you are very familiar with. Note your times and how you felt at the end of the workout.

Now do the same workout on your treadmill. You will probably feel just as fatigued or more so after your treadmill run.

er way to properly prepare yourself for your specific race conditions.

Does this mean you cannot ever do all of your runs on the treadmill? Absolutely not! Many runners, including some elite runners, have done most if not all of their training runs on the treadmill, with excellent results.

Several years ago, I did a rather unscientific experiment of one. For six months, I did all of my training runs on the treadmill in preparation for a January marathon. I did every run, from easy runs to goal pace long runs on the treadmill. The only runs I did outside were several 5K and 10K races.

I had done this race five times in the past and was very familiar with the course. My finishing time in the marathon was less than 3 minutes slower than my personal record in that race and was over 4 minutes faster than my worst performance.

During the race, I felt my fitness level was as high as it was with free range training. The only adverse effect I felt was considerable more fatigue in my calf muscles, which I believe was probably due to two factors.

• The running deck of the treadmill provided a much softer running surface. In the push off phase of my running stride, there was less resistance coming from the running surface and less stress being placed on my calf muscles. Even though I did several short races during training, this was not enough to adequately prepare my calf muscles for the roughly 42,000 contractions that they needed to perform during the marathon.

• The moving belt was doing some of the work required by my muscles. I ran with the treadmill elevated 1.5 percent, which theoretically compensated for the lack of wind resistance and the moving surface. This elevation required more action from my hamstrings to push off, but while my calf muscles were working a bit harder, they were still benefiting from the soft surface and moving belt.

My informal study of one does not stand alone. Don't forget about the cases of Dr. Christine Clark and Ingrid Kristiansen, who both ran highly successful marathons following training that was done nearly exclusively on the treadmill.

Will 100% treadmill training provide similar results in shorter race distances? Probably not. There is evidence that as running speed increases, the differences between treadmill training and free range running also increases. Remember the study that showed 36% difference in energy cost when sprinting on the track versus sprinting on the treadmill?

While there seems to be a large discrepancy between treadmill sprinting and track sprinting, studies also show very little difference when running speeds are slower. That would help explain the fabulous results obtained by elite marathon runners that trained on the treadmill. Using that data, it is reasonable to assume that when training for shorter events such as the 2 mile or 5K, you should plan on doing more of your training outside. It would also follow that 10K training requires a little less free range training and marathon training even less than that.

Taking into account the results of runners that I coach, my personal experience and the published accounts of several elite runners, it appears to be possible to do all of your marathon training on the treadmill with very little performance decrease. As the distance decreases and speed increases you should do more outside training. For most runners, I believe that without some free range training, there will be a decrease in race performance of between 1% and 3% in the 10K distance and a 2% to 5% decrease in the 5K distance. If you are training for short distances, such as the mile or less, you should do the majority of your quality pace training runs on the track.

How much outside running is necessary? Probably less than you may think. There has been very little research done in this area, but my observations have shown that you will adapt to outside running very quickly. As we already discussed, when training for the marathon, you can do nearly all of your runs on the treadmill with very little decrease in performance. When training for the 10K or 5K distances, it will depend upon where you are in your training cycle. Early in your cycle, when your training is more broad and less specific, you can do all of your runs on the treadmill. In the last 6 weeks of your cycle, it will become more important to include some free range running. For 10K runners, I would suggest a minimum of 1/3 of your training runs be done outside in the last 6 weeks of your cycle.

For 5K runners, a more appropriate level would be at least 1/2 of your training runs in the last 6 weeks be done on the road or track. It is also more critical to do your quality training runs outside. Easy or recovery runs can always be done on the treadmill. Concentrate on doing some of your lactate threshold workouts and speed work outside. Also try to do some of your hill training outside. If you have problems finding hills of sufficient length and incline in your area, then it is better to do your hill work on the treadmill.

8

Treadmill Training Programs

Successful training programs are a bit like snow-flakes. At first glance, they look similar, but when you take a closer look, no two are exactly alike. Each program is different because each individual runner is different. Every athlete is different physically, mentally and has distinctive goals and reasons for running. Some runners are in great shape and some are just starting to improve their fitness. Some are heavy, some are light. Some are running for fitness or to decrease weight, while others are competitive road or track racers. Because of the physical, mental and running goal differences, it is paramount that your training program be well chosen and specifically designed for your needs, goals and abilities.

It is a fact that all programs are different, but the overall make up of training programs are quite similar. They have both comparable principles and components. Training principles are the fundamental ideas that form the groundwork of nearly all productive training programs. Most programs include the following principles:

- Train consistently
- Start gently and make increases gradually
- Alternate hard and easy sessions
- Have a goal and train specifically for that goal
- Be flexible with your training schedule
- Train your mind as well as your body
- Train using multiple paces and workouts
- Don't overtrain
- Avoid junk miles - Work towards maximum results on minimum training

Training components are the different types of training runs. Each type of training run will target a particular energy producing system or muscle. For instance, endurance work improves your aerobic system, while speed work will increase the efficiency of your anaerobic system. Hill running will improve your running specific strength and power. Every training program will have some or all of the following components in various combinations:

- Endurance training
- Speed endurance/Tempo workouts
- Hill running
- Speedwork/Interval training
- Strength training
- Rest/Recovery

There is an almost limitless number of possible combinations of individual workouts within each of these components. This is where the art of coaching comes in.

Running is really a very simple sport, which is one of the reasons for its wide appeal. There are no complicated rules and no special equipment needed. The physiology of training and running is fairly easy to understand. The difficult part of training is putting together a mixture of all of the training components that will result in your best results.

I have tried to make this a little easier for you by developing a number of generic treadmill training programs for various experience levels and goals. These programs will work well for most runners, but keep in mind that they are very generic in nature. You should use these programs as a starting point and adapt them to your individual strengths, weaknesses, goals and circumstances. If you find some of the workouts too difficult, reduce either the pace or distance of the training run. If you feel that they are not challenging you enough, increase the pace, the distance or the number of repetitions. You should always be adjusting your training routine to keep pace with your increasing level of fitness. If you train consistently, you will gradually but regularly improve your fitness level and performance. If you do not make adjustments in your training program, your fitness increases will slow down or stop. You must always be challenging yourself. The challenge is what provokes your body to strengthen in response.

Before starting any exercise program, you should consult with your doctor to be sure you are cleared for intense activity. Any physical activity has the potential to cause injuries and/or serious medical conditions.

According to the American College of Sports Medicine, the minimum testing standard is the Physical Activity Readiness Questionnaire (PAR-Q). This is a questionnaire that is written to provide individuals a way to perform a simple self assessment of their readiness to engage in an exercise program.

The questionnaire asks the following seven questions:

- Has a doctor ever said that you have a heart condition and recommended only medically supervised activity?
- Do you have any chest pain brought on by physical activity?
- Have you developed chest pain in the past month?
- Do you tend to lose consciousness or fall over as a result of dizziness?
- Do you have a bone or joint problem that could be aggravated by the proposed physical activity?
- Has a doctor ever recommended medication for your blood pressure or heart condition?

- Are you aware through your own experience, or a doctor's advice, of other physical reasons against your exercising without medical supervision?

If you answered yes to one or more of the above questions, you must consult with your doctor before beginning any exercise program. If you answered no to all questions, you are reasonably assured that you are ready for an exercise program in which you will make gradual increases in the level of the activity. However, you should also consult with your doctor if any of the following apply to you:

- Over 40 years of age
- You are a smoker
- You have high blood pressure
- You have diabetes
- You have asthma
- You have lived a sedentary lifestyle
- You have a family history of cardiovascular disease
- You have high cholesterol

In addition to medical conditions, you must assess your musculoskeletal condition. If you have any prior injuries to your joints, any chronic back pain, any chronic joint pain or muscle injuries, check with your doctor before starting to run.

Use your own common sense. If you feel there is any possible risk at all, you should check with your doctor before running. It is much better to err on the safe side, than to suffer a serious injury or illness.

Choosing a program

The training programs have been developed for several categories. Below is a list of the various programs along with some guidelines to help you choose the program most appropriate for you. The most basic beginning program is the beginners program. The prerequisite for this program is the ability to walk for 30 minutes without stopping. If you are not able to walk for 30 minutes, you can build up to this level by walking every day. Start with 10 minutes at a comfortable pace and gradually build up to 30 minutes.

Beginners Program

This is a program for a beginning runner that has been mostly sedentary for the past several years. You must be able to walk at least 30 minutes without stopping before beginning this program. See above for suggestions for building up to this level. Choose this program if any of the following pertain to you:

- You have not run before or have not run in a long time.
- You are an apparently healthy person with no medical problems that would prohibit your participation in physical activity.
- You would like to begin a running and/or healthy lifestyle.
- You cannot run 2 miles without stopping.

Finish a 5K

This program will prepare you to finish a 5K race. Choose this program if:

- You can run at least 2 miles without stopping.
- You are new to racing.
- You want to complete a 5K race.

Finish a 10K

This program will prepare you to finish a 10K race. Choose this program if:

- You can run at least 3 miles without stopping.
- You are relatively new to racing or have not raced before.
- You want to complete a 10K race.

Weight Loss Program

This training program is designed to help lose weight and body fat. You must be able to run at least 2 miles before starting this program. Choose this program if:

- You can run at least 2 miles without stopping.
- Your primary running goal is to lose weight.
- You are not following a low carbohydrate diet.
- You have your doctors clearance to begin a running and strength training program that includes some high intensity running.
- You have a knowledge of safe weight lifting practices.

Fitness/Recreational Runner Program

Many athletes run only to improve their overall fitness and for recreation. This program is designed for fitness runners. Choose this program if:

- Fitness and health improvement is your primary goal.
- You are not interested in speed improvement.
- You do not compete in races or only occasionally enter local races.
- You run between 3 and 5 days per week.
- You are able to run at least 2 miles without stopping.

Finish a Half Marathon

This program will prepare a recreational runner to finish a half marathon. Choose this program if:

- You can run at least 6 miles without stopping.
- You are properly conditioned and medically cleared for the strenuous training required.

- Your goal is to finish a half marathon without a specific finishing time or pace.

Finish a Marathon

This program will prepare a recreational runner to finish a full marathon. Choose this program if:

- You can run at least 6 miles without stopping.
- You have the time to commit to the training required to finish a marathon.
- You are willing to commit fully to the training required.
- You are properly conditioned and medically cleared for the strenuous training required.
- Your goal is to finish a full marathon without a specific finishing time or pace.

Training for Competitive Runners

This program is designed for experienced competitive runners. Choose this program if:

- You have some competitive running experience.
- You want to improve your performance.
- You are conditioned for high intensity running.

Beginners Program

I'm sure that you have heard the phrase "no pain, no gain". You have probably also heard conflicting opinions on whether that axiom is true or false. It is, in reality, sometimes true and sometimes false. There will be times, later in your running life, when you may need to push yourself to uncomfortable levels in order to reach your potential. This is not one of those times. As a beginning runner, you should avoid exercising to the point of pain or extreme discomfort. You should feel fairly comfortable during all of your training runs and walks. There are two fundamental reasons for this.

• As a beginning runner, your muscles, joints and tendons have not been properly conditioned for high intensity running. If you assault your muscle and joints with an intense exercise that they are not ready for, you risk injury and will certainly suffer from extreme soreness and stiffness.
• You must enjoy running or you will probably not continue to engage in the activity. If you experience injury, soreness or are constantly in a state of discomfort, you will probably acquire a bad taste for running.

This program is designed for new runners that have little or no running experience. So, in order to keep your pace at a comfortable level and to allow your muscles and tendons to gradually adapt to this new stress, you will start out with walking and a walk/jog combination. Eventually you will run for 2 miles without stopping. If you are a new runner, that cannot run 2 miles without stopping, but feel that you are able to begin running right away, adjust your starting point in this program to the point at which you feel you can comfortably begin.

Workouts Included:

• The Freshman Starter

Treadmill Incorporation:

You may do any or all of these workouts on the treadmill. There is no disadvantage to doing all of these workouts on the treadmill. As mentioned in earlier chapters, beginning runners enjoy many advantages when doing these workouts on the treadmill. Advantages include injury prevention, exercise adherence and convenience.

Week 1

Day	Workout	Comments
1	Walk 30 minutes	Walk at a comfortable pace
2	Walk 30 minutes	Same workout as yesterday
3	The Freshman Starter - 30 minutes. Alternate between 5 minutes walk and 30 seconds jog.	Follow the 5/30 sequence for the entire 30 minutes
4	Rest	Take the day off
5	The Freshman Starter - 30 minutes. Alternate between 5 minutes walk and 30 seconds jog.	Same as day 3
6	The Freshman Starter - 30 minutes. Alternate between 5 minutes walk and 1 minute jog.	You make a slight increase in your jog time here
7	Rest	Rest

Week 2

Day	Workout	Comments
1	The Freshman Starter - 30 minutes. Alternate between 5 minutes walk and 1 minute jog.	Follow the sequence for the entire 30 minutes
2	The Freshman Starter - 30 minutes. Alternate between 5 minutes walk and 30 seconds jog.	Back to a 30 second jog for an easy day
3	The Freshman Starter - 30 minutes. Alternate between 5 minutes walk and 1 minute jog.	Return to 1 minute jog
4	Rest	Rest Day
5	The Freshman Starter - 30 minutes. Alternate between 5 minutes walk and 2 minute jog.	You increase to a 2 minute jog today
6	The Freshman Starter - 30 minutes. Alternate between 5 minutes walk and 2 minute jog.	Same as yesterday
7	Rest	Rest Day

Week 3

Day	Workout	Comments
1	The Freshman Starter - 30 minutes. Alternate between 5 minutes walk and 3 minutes jog	Another increase today. Keep your pace comfortable
2	The Freshman Starter - 30 minutes. Alternate between 5 minutes walk and 2 minutes jog	Back to a 2 minute jog for an easy day
3	The Freshman Starter - 30 minutes. Alternate between 5 minutes walk and 3 minutes jog	Same as day 1
4	Rest	Rest Day
5	The Freshman Starter - 30 minutes. Alternate between 5 minutes walk and 4 minutes jog.	Increase your jog to 4 minutes.
6	The Freshman Starter - 30 minutes. Alternate between 5 minutes walk and 4 minutes jog.	Same as yesterday
7	Rest	Rest Day

Week 4

Day	Workout	Comments
1	Walk for 30 minutes	An easy walk day for recovery
2	The Freshman Starter - 30 minutes. Alternate between 5 minutes walk and 5 minutes jog	You are now running as much as you are walking
3	The Freshman Starter - 30 minutes. Alternate between 5 minutes walk and 4 minutes jog	Back off a bit for recovery
4	Rest	Rest Day
5	The Freshman Starter - 30 minutes. Alternate between 4 minutes walk and 5 minutes jog	Now you will start to decrease the walk portion
6	The Freshman Starter - 30 minutes. Alternate between 4 minutes walk and 5 minutes jog	Same as yesterday
7	Rest	Rest Day

Week 5

Day	Workout	Comments
1	The Freshman Starter - 30 minutes. Alternate between 3 minutes walk and 5 minutes jog	Another decrease in your walk time.
2	The Freshman Starter - 30 minutes. Alternate between 4 minutes walk and 5 minutes jog	Easier workout today
3	The Freshman Starter - 30 minutes. Alternate between 3 minutes walk and 5 minutes jog	Same as day 1
4	Rest	Rest Day
5	The Freshman Starter - 30 minutes. Alternate between 2 minutes walk and 5 minute jog	Decrease to 2 minute walk today
6	The Freshman Starter - 30 minutes. Alternate between 2 minutes walk and 5 minute jog	Same as yesterday
7	Rest	Rest Day

Week 6

Day	Workout	Comments
1	The Freshman Starter - 30 minutes. Alternate between 1 minute walk and 5 minute jog	Decrease to a 1 minute walk
2	The Freshman Starter - 30 minutes. Alternate between 2 minute walk and 5 minute jog	Easier workout today
3	The Freshman Starter - 30 minutes. Alternate between 1 minute walk and 5 minute jog	Same as day 1
4	Rest	Rest Day
5	The Freshman Starter - 30 minutes. Alternate between 30 second walk and 5 minute jog	You are down to less than 1 minute of walking
6	The Freshman Starter - 30 minutes. Alternate between 30 second walk and 5 minute jog	Same as yesterday
7	Rest	Rest Day

Week 7

Day	Workout	Comments
1	Walk for 10 minutes. Then jog 2 x 1 mile repeats. Jog one mile, then walk for 5 minutes before jogging another mile	This will introduce you to the training you will do as a more advanced runner
2	The Freshman Starter - 30 minutes. Alternate between 30 seconds walk and 5 minute jog	
3	Walk for 10 minutes, then jog for 1.25 miles. Cool down with 10 minutes of walking	This is your longest run yet!
4	Rest	Rest Day
5	Walk for 10 minutes, then run 2 x 1 mile repeats. Cool down with 10 minutes of walking	Same as day 1
6	Walk for 10 minutes, then jog for 1.5 miles. Cool down with 10 minutes of walking	You have extended your run to 1.5 miles.
7	Rest	Rest Day

Week 8

Day	Workout	Comments
1	Walk for 10 minutes, then run 2 x 1 mile repeats. Cool down with 10 minutes of walking	
2	The Freshman Starter - 30 minutes. Alternate 30 seconds walk and 5 minute jog	
3	Walk for 10 minutes, then jog 1.75 miles. Cool down with a 10 minute walk	This is your longest run to date
4	Rest	Rest Day
5	Walk for 10 minutes, then run for 2 miles. Cool down with 10 minutes of walking	You are now running a full 2 miles without stopping
6	Walk for 10 minutes, then run 2.25 miles. Cool down with 10 minutes of walking	If you are still fatigued from yesterdays workout, skip this one and rest.
7	Rest	Rest Day

Finish a 5K

It is important to always have a goal in mind when running. For a beginning or recreational runner, that goal may be weight loss, fitness gains, stress reduction or a lifestyle change. Without a goal to work towards, your running can become stagnant and aimless. You may stop progressing or may even quit running. Racing provides goals even when your other goals may start to fade away.

A good choice for your first goal race is a 5K. This is a worthy selection for your first race because the distance is short and because it is the most common race distance. You can usually find a 5K race to participate in at any time of the year. This program is geared towards beginning runners that have little or no race experience. You must be able to run at least 2 miles without stopping before you undertake this training schedule. If you cannot run 2 miles, follow the beginning runners program before graduating to this one.

Workouts Included:

The Big Easy

Treadmill Incorporation:

You may do any or all of these workouts on the treadmill. There will be little or no physiological disadvantage to doing all of these runs on the treadmill. You will be training only to finish the race, not for performance. In later races, as your finishing time becomes more important, there will be some advantage to doing some runs outside on the roads or trails. But, for now, feel free to do all of your runs on the treadmill. Of course, you can also do any of these runs outside. It is up to you.

Week 1

Day	Workout	Comments
1	The Big Easy - 1 mile	Run at an easy pace
2	The Big Easy - 2 miles	Maintain an easy pace
3	Rest	Rest Day
4	The Big Easy - 2 miles	Same as day 2
5	The Big Easy - 2 miles	Easy pace
6	The Big Easy - 2 miles	Easy pace
7	Rest	Rest Day

Week 2

Day	Workout	Comments
1	The Big Easy - 2.25 miles	Small increase in mileage
2	The Big Easy - 2 miles	Back to 2 miles today
3	Rest	Rest Day
4	The Big Easy - 2.25 miles	Same as day 1
5	The Big Easy - 2 miles	
6	The Big Easy - 2.25 miles	All increases are gradual
7	Rest	Rest Day

Week 3

Day	Workout	Comments
1	The Big Easy - 2.25 miles	This mileage should feel easier
2	The Big Easy - 2 miles	
3	Rest	Rest Day
4	The Big Easy - 2.25 miles	Same as day 1
5	The Big Easy 2 miles	Same as day 2
6	The Big Easy - 3 miles	A small increase in mileage
7	Rest	Rest day

Week 4

Day	Workout	Comments
1	The Big Easy - 3 miles	Almost a full 5K distance
2	The Big Easy - 2 miles	Less mileage for an easy day
3	Rest	Rest Day
4	The Big Easy - 3 miles	Same as day 1
5	The Big Easy - 2 miles	Another easier day
6	The Big Easy - 3 miles	This should be getting easier
7	Rest	Rest Day

Week 5

Day	Workout	Comments
1	The Big Easy - 3.25 miles	This is more than a 5K
2	The Big Easy - 2 miles	Easy day
3	Rest	Rest Day
4	The Big Easy - 3 miles	
5	The Big Easy - 2 miles	
6	The Big Easy - 3.5 miles	This is your longest run
7	Rest	Rest Day

Week 6

Day	Workout	Comments
1	The Big Easy - 3.25 miles	
2	The Big Easy - 3 miles	You will start to decrease your mileage so your legs are fresh for the race
3	Rest	Rest Day
4	The Big Easy - 2 miles	
5	The Big Easy - 2 miles	
6	Rest	Rest Day
7	5K Race	Race Day - Have Fun

Finish a 10K

For a beginning/recreational runner, the 10K holds a lot of appeal. It is long enough to present a considerable challenge, but is still short enough that a beginner can prepare for it in a reasonable amount of time. As with the 5K, the popularity of the 10K makes it easy to find races during most times of the year.

It is best for a beginning runner to approach races progressively. Train for and complete a 5K first, then train for a 10K. This will allow your body to gradually adapt to the longer distances. While this is the preferred method, the 10K is short enough for a beginner to complete as their first race.

The prerequisite to starting this program is the ability to run at least 3 miles without stopping. If you cannot run 3 miles, complete the 5K training program, even if you are not going to run a 5K. After graduating from the 5K program you will be ready to start this training schedule. As with the beginners 5K program, this schedule will prepare you to finish a 10K race. It will not train you to race the 10K or to finish in a specific time or run at a specific pace. You should not worry about pace in your first race. Just concentrate on finishing and having fun. You will be working on pace and performance in subsequent training programs and races.

Workouts Included:

The Big Easy

Treadmill Incorporation:

You may do any or all of these workouts on the treadmill, with very little decrease in physiological benefits. When you begin to train for performance, some outside running will become more important.

Week 1

Day	Workout	Comments
1	The Big Easy - 2 miles	Keep your pace easy
2	The Big Easy - 3 miles	All increases will be gradual
3	Rest	Rest Day
4	The Big Easy - 2.5 miles	
5	The Big Easy - 3 miles	
6	The Big Easy - 3 miles	Same as yesterday
7	Rest	Rest Day

Week 2

Day	Workout	Comments
1	The Big Easy - 3.25 miles	A slight increase today
2	The Big Easy - 3 miles	Easy pace
3	Rest	Rest Day
4	The Big Easy - 3.25 miles	Same as day 1
5	The Big Easy - 3 miles	This mileage should be easy now
6	The Big Easy - 3.5 miles	Another small increase
7	Rest	Rest Day

Week 3

Day	Workout	Comments
1	The Big Easy - 3.5 miles	
2	The Big Easy - 3.5 miles	Same as yesterday
3	Rest	Rest Day
4	The Big Easy - 3.75 miles	More mileage today
5	The Big Easy - 3.25 miles	Easy pace
6	The Big Easy - 4 miles	Another small increase
7	Rest	Rest Day

Week 4

Day	Workout	Comments
1	The Big Easy - 4 miles	Easy pace
2	The Big Easy - 3 miles	Easy pace
3	Rest	Rest Day
4	The Big Easy - 4.25 miles	An increase in mileage today
5	The Big Easy - 3 miles	An easy day
6	The Big Easy - 4.5 miles	Another increase
7	Rest	Rest Day

Week 5

Day	Workout	Comments
1	The Big Easy - 4.5 miles	Keep your pace easy
2	The Big Easy - 3 miles	An easy day
3	Rest	Rest Day
4	The Big Easy - 4 miles	Remember - easy pace
5	The Big Easy - 3 miles	Easy day
6	The Big Easy - 5 miles	Your longest run to date
7	Rest	Rest Day

Week 6

Day	Workout	Comments
1	The Big Easy - 4 miles	This distance should be getting easier
2	The Big Easy - 3 miles	Easy day
3	Rest	Rest Day
4	The Big Easy - 3 miles	Another easy day
5	The Big Easy - 3 miles	Same as yesterday
6	The Big Easy - 5.5 miles	You will start doing one longer run per week
7	Rest	Rest Day

Week 7

Day	Workout	Comments
1	The Big Easy - 4 miles	Keep your pace comfortable
2	The Big Easy - 3 miles	Easy day
3	Rest	Rest Day
4	The Big Easy - 3 miles	Easy day
5	The Big Easy - 3 miles	Easy day
6	The Big Easy - 6 miles	Almost a full 10K
7	Rest	Rest Day

Week 8

Day	Workout	Comments
1	The Big Easy - 5 miles	Keep the pace easy
2	The Big Easy - 3 miles	Easy day
3	Rest	Rest Day
4	The Big Easy - 6.25 miles	You are now running just over the 10K distance
5	The Big Easy - 2 miles	You will decrease your mileage so that your legs are fresh and strong for the race
6	Rest	Rest Day
7	10K Race	Race Day

Weight Loss Program

It happens in January of each and every year. The attendance at athletic clubs soar. Exercise equipment sales go through the roof. Diets books become the most popular sellers in bookstores. Why does this happen? Because losing weight is the most common New Year's resolution. Weight loss is also one of the leading reasons that adults decide to start running. There is good reason for this. Running burns more calories than nearly any other form of exercise, trailing only cross country skiing.

Despite what the multi-billion dollar weight loss industry would like you to believe, the theory of weight loss is really quite simple. If you burn more calories than you take in, on a consistent basis, you will gradually lose weight. While the theory is simple, the practice of weight control can be much more difficult.

It takes a combination of cardiovascular exercise, strength training and diet modifications to have long term success with weight loss. The cardiovascular exercise, such as running, will burn calories and will also make changes in your body that make you a more efficient fat burner. Muscle mass is where most of the energy is burned in your body. That is why strength training is important. The strength exercises build more of the energy burning muscles. Finally, diet modifications are necessary. This is the trickiest part. You must slightly decrease the number of calories you are taking in, without compromising the nutritional needs of your exercising muscles. You do this by cutting portion sizes slightly, while maintaining a healthy, balanced diet that is high in complex carbohydrates, lean proteins, vegetables, fruits and essential fats. You should minimize simple carbohydrates and saturated fats. As a runner, you cannot engage in one of the popular, low carbohydrate diets while you are exercising. Carbohydrates are the primary fuel for exercise. If you are eliminating carbohydrates from your diet, you will not be able to exercise at the necessary level and will not gain the full benefits of running and strength training.

This program uses a 14 day schedule. This does not mean that you exercise for 14 days and then quit. You simply keep following the 14 day cycle of workouts for the duration of your program. This program is designed specifically for weight loss and does not prepare you for racing or long distance running. Most users of this type of program are interested only in weight loss and have little or no desire to become a distance runner or a road racer. If you do want to take up the sport of running, it is really not necessary to follow this program. The training schedules for competitive runners will also result in weight loss.

The prerequisite for this program is the ability to run 2 miles without stopping, your doctors clearance to begin a running program that includes some high intensity running and strength training, and knowledge of safe weight lifting practices.

If you cannot currently run 2 miles, complete the beginners program first. If you are not knowledgeable concerning proper weight lifting technique, I would suggest you have a personal trainer in your area give you some instruction. I have included some brief instructions of the strength training exercises, but it would be better if you were personally instructed concerning proper technique and safety when dealing with strength training.

Workouts Included:

The Fat Buster
The Strength Circuit
The Big Easy

Treadmill Incorporation:

You may do any or all of these workouts on the treadmill. The Strength Circuit workout should always be done on the treadmill, since you will be performing strength training exercises during the workout. The Fat Buster and The Big Easy may be performed on the treadmill or outside.

Weight Loss Schedule

Day	Workout	Comments
1	The Big Easy - 2 miles	This is an easy pace run
2	The Strength Circuit	Strength training will boost your metabolism
3	Rest	Rest Day
4	The Big Easy - 2.5 miles	More miles equals more calories burned
5	The Fat Buster	The higher intensity running will burn more calories and will improve your running speed.
6	The Big Easy - 3 miles	This easy pace run will improve your endurance
7	The Strength Circuit	Always use good form
8	The Big Easy - 3 miles	You can extend your miles gradually
9	Rest	Rest Day
10	The Fat Buster	When you increase your ability to run faster, you can burn more calories on your easy runs.
11	The Big Easy - 4 Miles	You will find you will be able to run faster at an easy pace
12	The Strength Circuit	Always do your strength exercises slowly and in control
13	The Big Easy - 3 miles	
14	The Fat Buster	

Continue this cycle for the duration of your program. As you become more fit, increase the distance of your easy runs. Do not make any sudden increases in mileage. If you increase your mileage too fast, you will risk injury. A good rule of thumb is to make no increases over 10%.

The higher intensity running you are doing with The Fat Buster workout, will improve your running speed. As your fitness level increases your running will begin to feel easier at all paces. So, you should always be adjusting your pace. You should be able to perform your easy runs at faster speeds, while maintaining the comfortable pace. The faster speed will equal more calories burned during your easy runs. Also adjust the speed of your higher intensity runs as your fitness level increases.

Fitness/Recreational Runner Program

This training program is intended for you weekend warriors out there. This is actually the most common type of runner. This runner exercises in order to improve their health/fitness levels, as a social activity or just for fun. This program is designed to improve your fitness level and get you in shape for the occasional local 5K or 10K. This training schedule uses mostly easy endurance runs, with a scattering of entry level speed workouts.

Before beginning this program, you should be able to run at least 2 miles without stopping. You should also have your doctors clearance for participating in a running program that includes some higher intensity running and some strength training.

Workouts Included:

The Big Easy
The Strength Circuit
The Aerobic Circuit
The Junk Eliminator
One Mile Repeats

Treadmill Incorporation:

Since racing is not typically a major goal of a fitness runner, all of these workouts may be done on the treadmill with no disadvantages. However, if you decide that you would like to enter a local race, you will be better prepared for it if you do a few of your runs outside on the road or trail. Once you have a race picked out, do 2 to 3 workouts outside in the 3 weeks before your race. That will help prepare your muscles and joints for the harder surfaces that you will encounter during the race.

Fitness/Recreational Runner Schedule

Day	Workout	Comments
1	The Big Easy - 2 miles	This is your typical daily run
2	The Big Easy - 3 miles	As you get fitter, increase the distance of your daily run
3	The Strength Circuit	Strength training will improve your overall fitness level
4	Off	Rest Day
5	The Junk Eliminator - 3 miles	This workout helps eliminate aimless running
6	The Big Easy 2 miles	Easy pace
7	The Aerobic Circuit	This is a great cross training workout that will improve your overall fitness
8	Off	Rest Day
9	The Big Easy - 3 miles	Easy pace
10	One Mile Repeats - 3 repeats	This is a higher intensity workout that will improve your speed endurance
11	The Big Easy - 3 miles	Easy pace
12	The Strength Circuit	Strength training once per week is a good starting point
13	The Big Easy - 3 miles	Easy pace
14	Off	Rest Day

Follow this sequence or one similar to it for the duration of your program. You will need to constantly adjust your paces and distances to keep up with your improved level of fitness.

Finish a Half Marathon

The half marathon distance has become more and more popular in recent years. For beginning runners it is a good stepping stone toward a full marathon. For more experienced runners it presents the challenge of a longer distance event with the need to sustain a quality pace for the entire distance.

Many marathon organizers around the world are starting to include a half marathon in their race weekend packages. There are many runners that want to participate in the excitement of a major marathon, but do not want to train for a full marathon. The half marathon give these runners the opportunity to participate in a long distance event with the "marathon atmosphere".

This training schedule is intended to prepare a recreational runner to finish a half marathon. There will be little emphasis on speed or pace. The goal of this program is to train a runner to finish the race comfortably. This training program will not prepare you to finish in a specific time or pace.

You should be able to run at least 6 miles without stopping before attempting this training program. If you cannot run 6 miles, complete the "Finish a 10K" program before continuing on to this one. You must also get medical clearance from your physician before beginning this or any other exercise program.

Workouts Included:

The Big Easy
Easy Marathon Run

Treadmill Incorporation:

You can do all of these workouts on the treadmill and get satisfactory results, but in order to prepare your muscles and tendons for the harder road surfaces you will be running on, it is advisable to do a couple runs on the road.

Week 1

Day	Workout	Comments
1	Rest	Rest
2	The Big Easy	4 Miles
3	The Big Easy	4 Miles
4	The Big Easy	3 Miles
5	The Big Easy	4 Miles
6	The Big Easy	3 Miles
7	The Big Easy	6 Miles

Week 2

Day	Workout	Comments
1	Rest	Rest
2	The Big Easy	4 Miles
3	The Big Easy	5 Miles
4	The Big Easy	4 Miles
5	The Big Easy	5 Miles
6	The Big Easy	3 Miles
7	The Big Easy	7 Miles

Week 3

Day	Workout	Comments
1	Rest	Rest
2	The Big Easy	4 Miles
3	The Big Easy	5 Miles
4	The Big Easy	4 Miles
5	The Big Easy	5 Miles
6	Rest	Rest
7	The Big Easy	8 Miles

Week 4

Day	Workout	Comments
1	Rest	Rest
2	The Big Easy	4 Miles
3	The Big Easy	5 Miles
4	The Big Easy	4 Miles
5	The Big Easy	6 Miles
6	The Big Easy	3 Miles
7	The Big Easy	9 Miles

Week 5

Day	Workout	Comments
1	Rest	Rest
2	The Big Easy	4 Miles
3	The Big Easy	6 Miles
4	The Big Easy	4 Miles
5	The Big Easy	6 Miles
6	Rest	Rest
7	The Big Easy	10 Miles

Week 6

Day	Workout	Comments
1	Rest	Rest
2	The Big Easy	4 Miles
3	The Big Easy	6 Miles
4	The Big Easy	5 Miles
5	The Big Easy	6 Miles
6	The Big Easy	3 Miles
7	The Big Easy	11 Miles

Week 7

Day	Workout	Comments
1	Rest	Rest
2	The Big Easy	4 Miles
3	The Big Easy	6 Miles
4	The Big Easy	5 Miles
5	The Big Easy	7 Miles
6	Rest	Rest
7	The Big Easy	8 Miles

Week 8

Day	Workout	Comments
1	Rest	Rest
2	The Big Easy	4 Miles
3	The Big Easy	6 Miles
4	The Big Easy	6 Miles
5	The Big Easy	7 Miles
6	The Big Easy	3 Miles
7	Easy Marathon Run	13 Miles

Week 9

Day	Workout	Comments
1	Rest	Rest
2	The Big Easy	4 Miles
3	The Big Easy	6 Miles
4	The Big Easy	5 Miles
5	The Big Easy	6 Miles
6	Rest	Rest
7	The Big Easy	8 Miles

Week 10

Day	Workout	Comments
1	Rest	Rest
2	The Big Easy	4 Miles
3	The Big Easy	6 Miles
4	The Big Easy	4 Miles
5	The Big Easy	7 Miles
6	The Big Easy	4 Miles
7	Easy Marathon Run	15 Miles

Week 11

Day	Workout	Comments
1	Rest	Rest
2	The Big Easy	4 Miles
3	The Big Easy	6 Miles
4	The Big Easy	5 Miles
5	The Big Easy	6 Miles
6	Rest	Rest
7	The Big Easy	10 Miles

Week 12

Day	Workout	Comments
1	Rest	Rest
2	The Big Easy	4 Miles
3	The Big Easy	6 Miles
4	The Big Easy	4 Miles
5	Rest	Rest
6	Rest	Rest
7	Race Day	13.1 Miles

Finish a Marathon

For many years, the marathon was an event reserved for only the fastest, most experienced runners. That started changing in the 1970's.

The first marathon boom of the 1970's brought many more runners into the world of the marathon. While the number of participants increased enormously, most of the marathoners were still accomplished athletes that were running competitively. They ran the marathon because they wanted to compete against others of their age group and their goal was to finish in the best time possible.

In the 1990's, another running boom appeared. This revolution, which may have been fueled, in part, by the incredible amount of publicity given to television star Oprah Winfrey's participation in the Marine Corps marathon, targeted several new groups. People now saw that a middle age person with very little athletic experience could also run a marathon. Finishing time became less important and just finishing became the goal. Participants began to train for and complete marathons for a variety of very valid reasons, including: weight loss, lifestyle change, goal setting, fitness, self improvement and dedication to a sick or deceased family member or friend.

This training program will prepare the more casual runner to finish a marathon. This program emphasizes easy running. There is very little attention paid to training for speed or pace. Therefore, this program will prepare you to finish the marathon, but will not get you ready to run a particular pace or finish in a specific time.

Before starting this program, you should be able to run at least 6 miles comfortably, without stopping. If you cannot run 6 miles, complete the "Finish a 10K" program before attempting this one. You must also get medical clearance before attempting to run the long distances required by this program.

Walking Breaks:

It is neither necessary nor advisable for inexperienced marathon runners to run throughout their long training runs. Take frequent walking breaks as needed. The walking breaks will give your muscles some valuable recovery time and will make completing these long workouts much easier. There are a number of walk/run patterns that you could follow. One possible pattern is to walk for one minute for each mile of running. You should also plan to take walking breaks during your actual race. A good way to incorporate walking breaks into your race is to walk for approximately one minute at each fluid station in the race.

Workouts Included:

The Big Easy
Easy Marathon Run

Treadmill Incorporation:

You can do all of these workouts on the treadmill and get satisfactory results, but in order to prepare your muscles and tendons for the harder road surfaces you will be running on, it is advisable to do a couple of runs on the road.

Prerequisite:

You should be able to run at least 6 miles before starting this program.

Week 1

Day	Workout	Comments
1	Rest	Rest
2	The Big Easy	4 Miles
3	The Big Easy	4 Miles
4	The Big Easy	3 Miles
5	The Big Easy	4 Miles
6	The Big Easy	3 Miles
7	The Big Easy	6 Miles

Week 2

Day	Workout	Comments
1	Rest	Rest
2	The Big Easy	4 Miles
3	The Big Easy	5 Miles
4	The Big Easy	4 Miles
5	The Big Easy	5 Miles
6	Rest	Rest
7	The Big Easy	8 Miles

Week 3

Day	Workout	Comments
1	Rest	Rest
2	The Big Easy	4 Miles
3	The Big Easy	5 Miles
4	The Big Easy	4 Miles
5	The Big Easy	6 Miles
6	The Big Easy	3 Miles
7	The Big Easy	10 Miles

Week 4

Day	Workout	Comments
1	Rest	Rest
2	The Big Easy	4 Miles
3	The Big Easy	5 Miles
4	The Big Easy	4 Miles
5	The Big Easy	5 Miles
6	Rest	Rest
7	Easy Marathon Run	12 Miles

Week 5

Day	Workout	Comments
1	Rest	Rest
2	The Big Easy	5 Miles
3	The Big Easy	5 Miles
4	The Big Easy	4 Miles
5	The Big Easy	6 Miles
6	The Big Easy	3 Miles
7	Easy Marathon Run	14 Miles

Week 6

Day	Workout	Comments
1	Rest	Rest
2	The Big Easy	4 Miles
3	The Big Easy	5 Miles
4	The Big Easy	5 Miles
5	The Big Easy	4 Miles
6	Rest	Rest
7	The Big Easy	8 Miles

Week 7

Day	Workout	Comments
1	Rest	Rest
2	The Big Easy	4 Miles
3	The Big Easy	5 Miles
4	The Big Easy	6 Miles
5	The Big Easy	4 Miles
6	The Big Easy	3 Miles
7	Easy Marathon Run	16 Miles

Week 8

Day	Workout	Comments
1	Rest	Rest
2	The Big Easy	4 Miles
3	The Big Easy	5 Miles
4	The Big Easy	4 Miles
5	The Big Easy	5 Miles
6	Rest	Rest
7	The Big Easy	10 Miles

Week 9

Day	Workout	Comments
1	Rest	Rest
2	The Big Easy	5 Miles
3	The Big Easy	5 Miles
4	The Big Easy	4 Miles
5	The Big Easy	6 Miles
6	The Big Easy	4 Miles
7	Easy Marathon Run	18 Miles

Week 10

Day	Workout	Comments
1	Rest	Rest
2	The Big Easy	5 Miles
3	The Big Easy	5 Miles
4	The Big Easy	4 Miles
5	The Big Easy	7 Miles
6	Rest	Rest
7	The Big Easy	10 Miles

Week 11

Day	Workout	Comments
1	Rest	Rest
2	The Big Easy	5 Miles
3	The Big Easy	5 Miles
4	The Big Easy	4 Miles
5	The Big Easy	5 Miles
6	The Big Easy	4 Miles
7	Easy Marathon Run	20 Miles

Week 12

Day	Workout	Comments
1	Rest	Rest
2	The Big Easy	5 Miles
3	The Big Easy	6 Miles
4	The Big Easy	5 Miles
5	The Big Easy	7 Miles
6	Rest	Rest
7	The Big Easy	8 Miles

Week 13

Day	Workout	Comments
1	Rest	Rest
2	The Big Easy	5 Miles
3	The Big Easy	6 Miles
4	The Big Easy	4 Miles
5	The Big Easy	8 Miles
6	The Big Easy	4 Miles
7	Easy Marathon Run	22 Miles

Week 14

Day	Workout	Comments
1	Rest	Rest
2	The Big Easy	5 Miles
3	The Big Easy	6 Miles
4	The Big Easy	5 Miles
5	The Big Easy	8 Miles
6	Rest	Rest
7	Easy Marathon Run	12 Miles

Week 15

Day	Workout	Comments
1	Rest	Rest
2	The Big Easy	5 Miles
3	The Big Easy	5 Miles
4	The Big Easy	4 Miles
5	The Big Easy	5 Miles
6	The Big Easy	6 Miles
7	The Big Easy	10 Miles

Week 16

Day	Workout	Comments
1	Rest	Rest
2	The Big Easy	6 Miles
3	The Big Easy	5 Miles
4	The Big Easy	4 Miles
5	Rest	Rest
6	Rest	Rest
7	Race Day	26.2 Miles

Training for Competitive Runners

If you are like most competitive runners, you are never far from race shape. Barring injury or illness, the typical competitive runner trains year round with some planned time off for recovery. A period of rest is a critical part of your training year. You will always have short periods of recovery following a race. The longer the race, the longer that immediate recovery period will be. Most runners will recover for 2 to 5 days following a 5K or 10K race and for 2 weeks or more following a marathon. In addition to the short periods of race recovery, it is a good idea to plan a recovery period of 2 to 4 weeks after your race season in order to restore the strength of both your body and your spirit, so that you are mentally and physically fresh and ready to run for the following race season.

It is after that planned period of rest, that you will want to rebuild and improve upon your base of endurance and strength that will support your training for the coming year.

This program is broken up into phases. The first phase is a pre-season schedule. This is commonly referred to as "base building" I do not like the term "base building" because it suggests that something must be built from the ground up. As I said earlier, competitive runners are never far from their base and never far from race shape. The pre-season training schedule is designed to refocus and strengthen the base that has already been built over years of consistent running.

The pre-season phase, as well as all other phases, is based on multi-pace training, and includes endurance, speed endurance and speed work. The emphasis will be on endurance training, but it is necessary to include both speed endurance and speed work so that you will maintain both your lactate threshold level and your footspeed.

The appropriate training schedule is very similar for all competitive runners. The big differences will be pace, distance and number of repetitions. Each schedule will have suggestions for adapting the program to your specific needs.

Following the pre-season schedule, there will be programs that will emphasize your goal distance from 5K to a full marathon. Training for distances from 5K to the marathon is really quite similar. Changes are made in long run length, repetition length and the percentage of speed workouts to endurance workouts. But, again, as a competitive runner, you are never far from race condition, no matter what the race distance is.

Each specific race distance program will have suggestions for three levels of runner. The three levels - freshman; intermediate and expert - are not distinguished by race times. Current race times will vary greatly even among expert runners. Other factors, such as age and natural ability will have an effect on the potential of each runner. The different levels are separated by the runners experience level and the amount of time and effort that is spent in training and racing

• Freshman competitor - This level of runner is fairly new to racing. They have been racing for a year or less. This runner will devote 5 to 6 days per week to training and has a weekly mileage of between 25 and 30 miles. This type of runner should be conditioned for moderately intense workouts and has some beginning strength training experience.

- Intermediate competitor - A runner at this level has been racing between 1 and 3 years. They will devote 6 to 7 days per week to training. Their weekly mileage will be between 30 and 50 miles. These runners should be conditioned for intense workouts and should be comfortable with strength training.
- Expert competitor - This is the highest level of competitive runner. These runners has been racing for 3 years or more and devotes 7 days per week to training. A runner at this level will usually run at least 40 miles per week and may run in excess of 100 miles per week. This type of runner should be conditioned for highly intense workouts and long runs of 23 to 28 miles. This athlete should be comfortable with strength training and plyometrics.

Pre-Season Schedule

Workouts Included:

The Big Easy
The Strength Circuit
The Cruiser
One Mile Repeats
400 Meter Repeats
Hill Progression

Treadmill Incorporation:

This is a pre-season schedule, so there will be few, if any, races involved. So, during this phase, you may do all of these workouts on the treadmill. As a competitive runner, you must always be concerned with the rule of specificity, which means that you should train specifically for your goal. Your races will be run on firmer surfaces than the treadmill. Even though you will be doing very little racing in this phase, you should try to do some of your training runs on the road, track or trail. Try to do at least a couple of each type of run outside. If weather or other conditions in your area make this difficult, go ahead and do all of these runs on the treadmill. You will still get satisfactory results. It will become more important to do some training runs outside during the next phase.

Week 1

Day	Workout	Comments
1	The Big Easy or Rest	Freshman level take the day off, intermediate and expert levels do 3 miles
2	The Big Easy	All Levels - 3 miles
3	The Big Easy	Freshman level do 3 miles, intermediate level and expert level do 4 miles
4	400 meter repeats	Freshman Level do 3 repeats Intermediate and expert levels do 4 repeats
5	The Big Easy	Freshman level do 3 miles. Intermediate and expert levels do 4 miles.
6	The Strength Circuit	You also need to begin working on overall strength
7	The Big Easy	Freshman and intermediate level do 4 miles, expert level do 5 miles.

Week 2

Day	Workout	Comments
1	The Big Easy or Rest	Freshman level take the day off, intermediate and expert levels do 4 miles
2	The Big Easy	Freshman level do 3 miles, intermediate level do 4 miles, expert level do 5 miles
3	The Big Easy	Freshman level do 4 miles, intermediate level do 5 miles, expert level do 6 miles
4	400 meter repeats	Freshman level do 4 repeats, intermediate and expert level do 5 repeats
5	The Big Easy	Freshman level do 3 miles, intermediate level do 5 miles, expert level do 6 miles
6	The Big Easy	Freshman level do 4 miles, intermediate level do 5 miles, expert level do 6 miles
7	The Big Easy	Freshman level do 5 miles, intermediate level do 6 miles, expert level do 7 miles

Week 3

Day	Workout	Comments
1	The Big Easy or Rest	Freshman level take the day off, intermediate and expert level do 5 miles
2	The Big Easy	Freshman level do 4 miles, intermediate level do 5 miles, expert level do 6 miles
3	The Big Easy	Freshman level do 4 miles, intermediate level do 6 miles, expert level do 7 miles
4	400 meter repeats	Freshman level do 4 repeats, intermediate level do 5 repeats, expert level do 6 repeats
5	The Big Easy	Freshman level do 4 miles, intermediate level do 6 miles, expert level do 7 miles
6	The Strength Circuit	All levels do one circuit
7	The Big Easy	Freshman level do 5 miles, intermediate level do 6 miles, expert level do 8 miles

Week 4

Day	Workout	Comments
1	The Big Easy or Rest	Freshman level take the day off, intermediate and expert levels do 6 miles.
2	The Cruiser	All levels do 3 miles
3	The Big Easy - 5 miles	Freshman level do 5 miles, intermediate level do 6 miles, expert level do 7 miles
4	400 meter repeats	Freshman level do 4 repeats, intermediate level do 5 repeats, expert level do 6 repeats
5	The Big Easy	Freshman level do 5 miles, intermediate level do 6 miles, expert level do 8 miles
6	The Big Easy	Freshman level do 5 miles, intermediate level do 6 miles, expert level do 7 miles
7	The Big Easy	Freshman level do 6 miles, intermediate level do 7 miles, expert level do 9 miles

Week 5

Day	Workout	Comments
1	The Big Easy or Rest	Freshman level take the day off, intermediate level do 6 miles, expert level do 7 miles
2	One Mile Repeats	All levels do 3 x 1 mile repeats
3	The Big Easy	Freshman level do 5 miles, intermediate level do 6 miles, expert level do 7 miles
4	400 meter repeats	Freshman level do 4 repeats, intermediate level do 5 repeats, expert level do 6 repeats
5	The Big Easy	Freshman level do 6 miles, intermediate level do 7 miles, expert level do 8 miles
6	The Strength Circuit	All levels do one circuit
7	The Big Easy	Freshman level do 7 miles, intermediate level do 8 miles, expert level do 10 miles

Week 6

Day	Workout	Comments
1	The Big Easy or Rest	Freshman level take the day off, intermediate level do 6 miles, expert level do 7 miles
2	The Cruiser	Freshman level do 3 miles, intermediate and expert level do 4 miles
3	The Big Easy	Freshman level do 6 miles, intermediate level do 7 miles, expert level do 8 miles
4	400 meter repeats	Freshman level do 4 repeats, intermediate level do 5 repeats, expert level do 6 repeats
5	The Big Easy	Freshman level do 7 miles, intermediate level do 8 miles, expert level do 9 miles
6	Hill Progression	All levels do one repeat
7	The Big Easy	Freshman level do 8 miles, intermediate level do 9 miles, expert level do 12 miles

Week 7

Day	Workout	Comments
1	The Big Easy or Rest	Freshman level take the day off, intermediate level do 6 miles expert level do 7 miles
2	One Mile Repeats	All levels do 4 x 1 mile repeats
3	The Big Easy	Freshman level do 6 miles, intermediate level do 8 miles, expert level do 10 miles
4	400 meter repeats	Freshman level do 4 repeats, intermediate level do 5 repeats, expert level do 6 repeats
5	The Big Easy	Freshman level do 7 miles, intermediate level do 9 miles, expert level do 10 miles
6	The Strength Circuit	All levels do 1 circuit
7	The Big Easy	Freshman level do 9 miles, intermediate level do 10 miles, expert level do 13 miles

Week 8

Day	Workout	Comments
1	The Big Easy or Rest	Freshman level take the day off, intermediate level do 6 miles, expert level do 8 miles
2	The Cruiser	Freshman level do 3 miles, intermediate level do 4 miles, expert level do 6 miles
3	The Big Easy	Freshman level do 7 miles, intermediate level do 9 miles, expert level do 11 miles
4	400 meter repeats	Freshman level do 4 repeats, intermediate level do 5 repeats, expert level do 6 repeats
5	The Big Easy	Freshman level do 8 miles, intermediate level do 10 miles, expert level do 11 miles
6	Hill Progression	All levels do one repeat
7	The Big Easy	Freshman level do 10 miles, intermediate level do 12 miles, expert level do 15 miles

5K Competitive Program

Workouts Included:

The Big Easy
The Cruiser
400 Meter Repeats
Hill Progression
Long Run Fartlek
Rolling Hills
One Mile Repeats
400 Meter Repeats with a Float
Pike's Peak
5K Long Run
800 Meter Repeats
Marathon Madness
The Hill Climb
800 Meter Repeats Increasing Pace
The Miracle Miles
Hill Blasters
5K Change of Pace
5K Hill Simulator
20 Minute Repeats
5 x 3 Minute Repeats

Treadmill Incorporation:

As you get closer to competing in your goal race or race season, you should begin to train as specifically as possible. For this reason, you should try to do several of your workouts on the road, trail or track. At this point in your training, most of your easy, recovery runs can be done on the treadmill with little or no adverse training effects. Your speed and speed endurance work should be done, at least partly, outside.

If you have hills in your area, try to do half of your hill workouts, outside on the hills. Of course, if you do not have hills in your area, do all hillwork on the treadmill. Can a competitive runner do all of their workouts on the tread-mill? This depends upon each individual runners goal.

You can do all of your training runs on the treadmill and get very good results. But, you will probably not run the absolute best time that you are capable of. If those precious seconds are important to you, it would be wise to perform some of your runs outside. The most important time to do outside running is in the last 5 to 6 weeks before your main goal race. Try to do at least 1/2 of your quality training runs outside during that period.

Prerequisite:

Before beginning this program you should complete the pre-season build up or have a sufficient base of fitness already in place.

Week 1

Day	Workout	Comments
1	The Big Easy	All levels do 6 miles
2	The Cruiser	Freshman level do 3 miles, intermediate and advanced level do 4 miles
3	The Big Easy	All levels do 6 miles
4	400 meter repeats	Freshman level do 4 repeats, intermediate level do 5 repeats, expert level do 6 repeats
5	The Big Easy	All levels do 6 miles
6	Hill Progression	All levels do one full workout
7	Long Run Fartlek	All levels do 10 miles

Week 2

Day	Workout	Comments
1	The Big Easy or Rest	Freshman level take the day off, intermediate and expert level do 6 miles
2	The Cruiser	Freshman level do 3 miles, intermediate do 5 miles, expert level do 6 miles
3	The Big Easy	Freshman and intermediate level do 6 miles, expert level do 7 miles
4	400 meter repeats	Freshman level do 5 repeats, intermediate level do 6 repeats, expert level do 8 repeats
5	The Big Easy	All levels do 6 miles
6	Rolling Hills	All levels do one full workout
7	The Big Easy	Freshman level do 8 miles, intermediate level do 10 miles, expert level do 12 miles

Week 3

Day	Workout	Comments
1	The Big Easy or Rest	Freshman level rest, intermediate and expert level do 6 miles
2	One Mile Repeats	Freshman level do 3 repeats, intermediate level do 4 repeats, expert level do 5 repeats
3	The Big Easy	Freshman level do 6 miles, intermediate level do 7 miles, expert level do 8 miles
4	400 meter repeats with a float	Freshman level do 4 repeats, intermediate level do 6 repeats, expert level do 8 repeats
5	The Big Easy	All levels do 6 miles
6	Pike's Peak	All levels do one full workout
7	5K Long Run	All levels do one full workout

Week 4

Day	Workout	Comments
1	The Big Easy or Rest	Freshman level rest, intermediate and expert level do 6 miles
2	Marathon Madness	Freshman level do 3 miles, intermediate level do 4 miles, expert level do 5 miles
3	The Big Easy	All levels do 6 miles
4	800 Meter Repeats	Freshman level do 4 repeats, intermediate level do 5 repeats, expert level do 6 repeats
5	The Big Easy	All levels do 6 miles
6	The Hill Climb	Freshman level do 3 miles, intermediate level do 4 miles, expert level do 5 miles
7	The Big Easy	All levels do 10 miles

Week 5

Day	Workout	Comments
1	The Big Easy or Rest	Freshman level take the day off, intermediate and expert level do 6 miles
2	The Miracle Miles	All levels do one full workout
3	The Big Easy	All levels do 6 miles
4	800 meter repeats increasing pace	Freshman level do 4 repeats, intermediate level do 5 repeats, expert level do 6 repeats
5	The Big Easy	All levels do 6 miles
6	Hill Blasters	All levels do one full workout
7	5K Long Run	All levels do one full workout

Week 6

Day	Workout	Comments
1	The Big Easy or Rest	Freshman level rest, intermediate and expert level do 4 miles
2	One Mile Repeats	Freshman level do 4 repeats, intermediate level do 5 repeats, expert level do 6 repeats
3	The Big Easy	All levels do 4 miles
4	5K Change of Pace	All levels do one full workout
5	Rest	All levels rest
6	5K Hill Simulator	All levels do one full workout
7	The Big Easy	All levels do 10 miles

Week 7

Day	Workout	Comments
1	The Big Easy or Rest	Freshman level rest, intermediate and expert level do 6 miles
2	20 minute repeats	All levels do two repeats
3	The Big Easy	All levels do 6 miles
4	5 x 3 minute repeats	All levels do one full workout
5	The Big Easy	All levels do 6 miles
6	The Hill Climb	Freshman level do 4 miles, intermediate level do 5 miles, expert level do 6 miles
7	5K Long Run	All levels do one full workout

Week 8

Day	Workout	Comments
1	The Big Easy or Rest	Freshman level rest, intermediate and expert level do 5 miles
2	The Cruiser	Freshman level do 3 miles, intermediate level do 4 miles, expert level do 5 miles
3	Rest	All levels rest
4	400 meter repeats with a float	Freshman level do 4 repeats, intermediate level do 5 repeats, expert level do 6 repeats
5	The Big Easy	All levels do 4 miles
6	Rest	All levels rest
7	5K Race	Race Day

10K Competitive Program

Workouts Included:

The Big Easy
The Cruiser
400 Meter Repeats
Hill Progression
Long Run Fartlek
Rolling Hills
One Mile Repeats
400 Meter Repeats with a Float
Pike's Peak
800 Meter Repeats
Marathon Madness
The Hill Climb
800 Meter Repeats Increasing Pace
The Miracle Miles
Hill Blasters
20 Minute Repeats
5 x 3 Minute Repeats
10K Long Run
Two Mile Repeats
3 x 1 Mile repeats
LT Ladder
LT Pyramid
5K Repeats

Treadmill Incorporation:

Advice for incorporating the treadmill into your competitive 10K training is similar to that of the 5K. You can do all of the workouts on the treadmill and get satisfactory results. But, in order to be totally prepared for a 10K road race, you should try to do at least some free range running. This becomes more important as you get closer to your race or race season. Early in your training schedule you will be able to do all of your runs on the treadmill without any significant disadvantages. As you progress through your training cycle and get closer to your race, you should begin to train more specifically. That means doing more training runs outside. During the last 6 weeks of your program, try to do at least 1/3 of each type of workout, outside on the track, road or trail. As with all of the training programs, you can do all of your runs on the treadmill and get satisfactory results, but if you want to run at your top level, you should do some of your workouts on the road, trail or track.

Prerequisite:

Before beginning this program you should complete the pre-season build up or have a sufficient base of fitness already in place.

Week 1

Day	Workout	Comments
1	The Big Easy	All levels do 6 miles
2	The Cruiser	Freshman level do 3 miles, intermediate and advanced levels do 4 miles
3	The Big Easy	All levels do 6 miles
4	400 meter repeats	Freshman level do 4 repeats, intermediate level do 5 repeats, expert level do 6 repeats
5	The Big Easy	All levels do 6 miles
6	Hill Progression	All levels do one full workout
7	Long Run Fartlek	All levels do 10 miles

Week 2

Day	Workout	Comments
1	The Big Easy or Rest	Freshman level take the day off, intermediate and expert levels do 6 miles
2	The Cruiser	Freshman level do 3 miles, intermediate level do 5 miles, expert level do 6 miles
3	The Big Easy	Freshman and intermediate level do 6 miles, expert level do 7 miles
4	400 meter repeats	Freshman level do 5 repeats, intermediate level do 6 repeats, expert level do 8 repeats
5	The Big Easy	All levels do 6 miles
6	Rolling Hills	All levels do one full workout
7	The Big Easy	Freshman level do 8 miles, intermediate level do 10 miles, expert level do 12 miles

Week 3

Day	Workout	Comments
1	The Big Easy or Rest	Freshman level take the day off, intermediate and expert level do 6 miles
2	One Mile Repeats	Freshman level do 3 repeats, intermediate level do 4 repeats, expert level do 5 repeats
3	The Big Easy	Freshman level do 6 miles, intermediate level do 7 miles, expert level do 8 miles
4	400 meter repeats with a float	Freshman level do 4 repeats, intermediate level do 6 repeats, expert level do 8 repeats
5	The Big Easy	All levels do 6 miles
6	Pike's Peak	All levels do one full workout
7	10K Long Run	All levels do one full workout

Week 4

Day	Workout	Comments
1	The Big Easy or Rest	Freshman level rest, intermediate and expert level do 6 miles
2	Marathon Madness	Freshman level do 3 miles, intermediate level do 5 miles, expert level do 6 miles
3	The Big Easy	All levels do 6 miles
4	800 meter repeats	Freshman level do 4 repeats, intermediate level do 5 repeats, expert level do 6 repeats
5	The Big Easy	All levels do 6 miles
6	The Hill Climb	Freshman level do 3 miles, intermediate level do 4 miles, expert level do 5 miles
7	The Big Easy	All levels do 10 miles

Week 5

Day	Workout	Comments
1	The Big Easy or Rest	Freshman level take the day off, intermediate and expert level do 6 miles
2	Two Mile Repeats	All levels do 3 repeats
3	The Big Easy	All levels do 6 miles
4	800 meter repeats increasing pace	Freshman level do 4 repeats, intermediate level do 5 repeats, expert level do 6 repeats
5	The Big Easy	All levels do 6 miles
6	Hill Blasters	All levels do one full workout
7	10K Long Run	All levels do one full workout

Week 6

Day	Workout	Comments
1	The Big Easy or Rest	Freshman level take the day off, intermediate and expert level do 4 miles
2	20 Minute Repeats	All levels do 2 repeats
3	The Big Easy	All levels do 4 miles
4	3 x 1 mile repeats	All levels do one full workout
5	Rest	All levels rest
6	Rolling Hills	All levels do one full workout
7	The Big Easy	All levels do 10 miles

Week 7

Day	Workout	Comments
1	The Big Easy or Rest	Freshman level take the day off, intermediate and expert level do 6 miles
2	LT Ladder	All levels do two ladders
3	The Big Easy	All levels do 6 miles
4	5 x 3 minute repeats	All levels do one full workout
5	The Big Easy	All levels do 6 miles
6	The Hill Climb	Freshman level do 4 miles, intermediate level do 5 miles, expert level do 6 miles
7	10K Long Run	All levels do one full workout

Week 8

Day	Workout	Comments
1	The Big Easy or Rest	Freshman level rest, intermediate and expert level do 6 miles
2	LT Pyramid	All levels do one workout
3	The Big Easy	Freshman level do 6 miles, intermediate and expert level do 7 miles
4	5 x 3 minute repeats	All levels do one full workout
5	The Big Easy	All levels do 6 miles
6	Rolling Hills	All levels do one full workout
7	The Big Easy	Freshman level do 10 miles, intermediate level do 12 miles, expert level do 14 miles

Week 9

Day	Workout	Comments
1	The Big Easy or Rest	Freshman level rest, intermediate and expert level do 6 miles
2	5K repeats	All levels do 2 repeats
3	The Big Easy	All levels do 6 miles
4	5 x 3 minute repeats	All levels do one full workout
5	The Big Easy	All levels do 6 miles
6	Hill Fartlek	All levels do 6 miles
7	The Big Easy	All levels do 10 miles

Week 10

Day	Workout	Comments
1	The Big Easy or Rest	Freshman level rest, intermediate and expert level do 5 miles
2	The Cruiser	Freshman level do 4 miles, intermediate level do 5 miles, expert level do 6 miles
3	Rest	All levels rest
4	800 meter repeats increasing pace	Freshman level do 4 repeats, intermediate level do 5 repeats, expert level do 6 repeats
5	The Big Easy	All levels do 5 miles
6	Rest	All levels rest
7	10K Race	Race Day

Half Marathon Competitive Program

Workouts Included:

The Big Easy
The Cruiser
400 Meter Repeats
Hill Fartlek
Easy Marathon Run
400 Meter Repeats with a Float
The Foothills
LT Pyramid
Rolling Hills
800 Meter Repeats
The Miracle Miles
800 Meter Repeats Increasing Pace
Marathon Mimic
Marathon Mimic with a Kick

LT Superset
Hill Progression
2 Mile Repeats
Speed Pyramid
Hill Blasters
20 Minute Repeats
3 x 1 Mile Repeats
Hill Climb
5 x 3 Minute Repeats
5K Repeats

Treadmill Incorporation:

As the distance of your goal race increases and your sustainable racing speed decreases, there are less differences between the benefits of treadmill training and free range training. Because of this, the half marathon distance requires less outdoor running than 5K or 10K training. As with all race distances, it becomes more important to include some road or track training in the last 6 weeks of your training program. During the last 6 weeks of your program, try to do at least 1/4 of each type of workout, outside on the track, road or trail. As with all of the training programs, you can do all of your runs on the treadmill and get satisfactory results, but if you want to run at your top level, you should do some of your workouts on the road, trail or track.

Prerequisite:

Before beginning this program you should complete the pre-season build up or have a sufficient base of fitness already in place.

Week 1

Day	Workout	Comments
1	The Big Easy or Rest	Freshman level take the day off, intermediate and expert level do 6 miles
2	The Cruiser	Freshman level do 4 miles, intermediate level do 5 miles, expert level do 6 miles
3	The Big Easy	All levels do 6 miles
4	400 Meter Repeats	Freshman level do 6 repeats, intermediate level do 8 repeats, expert level do 10 repeats
5	The Big Easy	All levels do 6 miles
6	Hill Fartlek	All levels do 3 miles
7	The Big Easy	Freshman level do 10 miles, intermediate level do 11 miles, expert level do 12 miles.

Week 2

Day	Workout	Comments
1	The Big Easy or Rest	Freshman level rest, intermediate and expert level do 6 miles.
2	The Cruiser	Freshman level do 5 miles, intermediate level do 6 miles, expert level do 7 miles
3	The Big Easy	All levels do 6 miles
4	400 Meter Repeats with a Float	Freshman level do 6 repeats, intermediate level do 8 repeats, expert level do 10 repeats
5	The Big Easy	All levels do 6 miles
6	The Foothills	All levels do one workout
7	The Big Easy	Freshman level do 7 miles, intermediate level do 9 miles, expert level do 10 miles

Week 3

Day	Workout	Comments
1	The Big Easy or Rest	Freshman level rest, intermediate and expert level do 6 miles
2	LT Pyramid	Freshman level do 1 pyramid, intermediate and expert level do 2 pyramids
3	The Big Easy	Freshman level do 6 miles, intermediate level do 7 miles, expert level do 8 miles
4	400 Meter Repeats with a Float	Freshman level do 8 repeats, intermediate level do 10 repeats, expert level do 12 repeats
5	The Big Easy	All levels do 6 miles
6	Rolling Hills	All levels do one workout
7	Easy Marathon Run	Freshman level do 11 miles. Intermediate level do 12 miles, expert level do 13 miles.

Week 4

Day	Workout	Comments
1	The Big Easy or Rest	Freshman level rest, intermediate and expert level do 6 miles
2	LT Pyramid	Freshman level do 2 pyramids, intermediate and expert levels do 3 pyramids
3	The Big Easy	Freshman level do 6 miles, intermediate level do 7 miles, expert level do 8 miles
4	800 Meter Repeats	Freshman level do 3 repeats, intermediate level do 4 repeats, expert level do 6 repeats
5	The Big Easy	All levels do 6 miles
6	Hill Fartlek	Freshman level do 3 miles, intermediate level do 4 miles, expert level do 5 miles
7	Easy Marathon Run	Freshman level do 9 miles, intermediate level do 10 miles, expert level do 11 miles

Week 5

Day	Workout	Comments
1	The Big Easy or Rest	Freshman level take the day off, intermediate and expert level do 6 miles
2	The Miracle Miles	All levels do one workout
3	The Big Easy	Freshman level do 7 miles, intermediate level do 8 miles, expert level do 9 miles
4	800 Meter Repeats Increasing Pace	Freshman level do 3 repeats, intermediate level do 4 repeats, expert level do 6 repeats
5	The Big Easy	All levels do 6 miles
6	The Foothills	All levels do one workout
7	Marathon Mimic	Freshman level do 12 miles with 6 at an easy pace followed by 6 at goal race pace. Intermediate level do 13 miles with 6 miles at an easy pace and 7 at goal race pace. Expert level do 14 miles with 6 miles at an easy pace followed by 8 at goal race pace

Week 6

Day	Workout	Comments
1	The Big Easy or Rest	Freshman level rest, intermediate and expert level do 6 miles
2	LT Superset	Freshman level do 1 superset, intermediate level do 2 supersets, expert level do 3 supersets.
3	The Big Easy	Freshman level do 7 miles, intermediate level do 8 miles, expert level do 10 miles
4	800 Meter Repeats Increasing Pace	Freshman level do 3 repeats, intermediate level do 5 repeats, expert level do 7 repeats
5	The Big Easy	All levels do 6 miles
6	Hill Progression	All levels do one workout
7	Easy Marathon Run	Freshman level do 12 miles, intermediate level do 13 miles, expert level do 15 miles

Week 7

Day	Workout	Comments
1	The Big Easy or Rest	Freshman level rest, intermediate and expert level do 6 miles
2	LT Superset	Freshman level do 2 supersets, intermediate level do 3 supersets, expert level do 4 supersets
3	The Big Easy	Freshman level do 7 miles, intermediated level do 8 miles, expert level do 10 miles
4	800 Meter Repeats Increasing Pace	Freshman level do 4 repeats, intermediate level do 6 repeats, expert level do 8 repeats
5	The Big Easy	All levels do 6 miles
6	Hill Fartlek	Freshman level do 3 miles, intermediate level do 4 miles, expert level do 5 miles
7	Marathon Mimic	Freshman level do 12 miles with 5 at an easy pace followed by 7 at goal race pace. Intermediate level do 14 miles with 6 miles at an easy pace and 8 at goal race pace. Expert level do 16 miles with 7 miles at an easy pace and 9 at goal race pace

Week 8

Day	Workout	Comments
1	Rest	All levels rest
2	2 Mile Repeats	Freshman level do 3 repeats, intermediate and expert level do 4 repeats
3	The Big Easy	Freshman level do 6 miles, intermediate level do 7 miles, expert level do 8 miles
4	Speed Pyramid	All levels do one workout
5	Rest	All levels rest
6	Hill Blasters	All levels do one workout
7	Easy Marathon Run	Freshman level do 13 miles, intermediate level do 15 miles, expert level do 17 miles

Week 9

Day	Workout	Comments
1	The Big Easy or Rest	Freshman level rest, intermediate and expert level do 6 miles
2	20 Minute Repeats	All levels do 2 repeats
3	The Big Easy	Freshman level do 7 miles, intermediate level do 8 miles, expert level do 10 miles
4	3 x 1 Mile Repeats	All levels do one workout
5	The Big Easy	All levels do 6 miles
6	The Hill Climb	Freshman level do 2 miles, intermediate level do 3 miles, expert level do 5 miles
7	Marathon Mimic	Freshman level do 14 miles with 6 at an easy pace followed by 8 at goal race pace. Intermediate level do 16 miles with 7 at an easy pace followed by 9 at goal race pace. Expert level do 18 miles with 8 miles at an easy pace followed by 10 at goal race pace

Week 10

Day	Workout	Comments
1	Rest	All levels rest
2	The Cruiser	Freshman level do 6 miles, intermediate level do 7 miles, expert level do 8 miles
3	The Big Easy	Freshman level do 6 miles, intermediate level do 7 miles, expert level do 8 miles
4	5 x 3 Minute Repeats	All levels do one workout
5	The Big Easy	All levels do 6 miles
6	Rest	Rest
7	Easy Marathon Run	Freshman level do 12 miles, intermediate level do 13 miles, expert level do 14 miles.

Week 11

Day	Workout	Comments
1	The Big Easy or Rest	Freshman level rest, intermediate and expert level do 6 miles
2	5K Repeats	All levels do 2 repeats
3	The Big Easy	Freshman level do 7 miles, intermediate level do 8 miles, expert level do 10 miles
4	3 x 1 Mile Repeats	All levels do one workout
5	The Big Easy	All levels do 6 miles
6	The Hill Climb	Freshman level do 3 miles, intermediate level do 5 miles, expert level do 7 miles
7	Marathon Mimic With a Kick	Freshman level do 14 miles with 6 at an easy pace followed by 7 at goal race pace and 1 at 10K pace. Intermediate level do 16 miles with 7 at an easy pace followed by 8 at goal race pace and 1 at 10K pace. Expert level do 18 miles with 8 miles at an easy pace, followed by 8 at goal race pace and 2 at 10K pace

Week 12

Day	Workout	Comments
1	Rest	All levels rest
2	The Cruiser	All levels do 5 miles
3	The Big Easy	All levels do 5 miles
4	Speed Pyramid	All levels do one workout
5	The Big Easy	All levels do 6 miles
6	Rest	Rest
7	Race Day	13.1 Miles at race pace

Marathon Competitive Program

Workouts Included:

The Big Easy
The Cruiser
400 Meter Repeats
Hill Fartlek
Easy Marathon Run
400 Meter Repeats with a Float
The Foothills
LT Pyramid
Rolling Hills
Marathon in the Middle
800 Meter Repeats
The Miracle Miles
800 Meter Repeats Increasing Pace
Marathon Mimic
Marathon Mimic with a Kick
LT Superset
Hill Progression
2 Mile Repeats
Speed Pyramid
Hill Blasters
20 Minute Repeats
3 x 1 Mile Repeats
Hill Climb
5 x 3 Minute Repeats
5K Repeats
Marathon Madness
Pike's Peak

Treadmill Incorporation:

The results you can achieve with treadmill training for a marathon is somewhat surprising and contrary to what most runners believe. Common sense would tell you that since you are taking approximately 42,000 steps on asphalt, concrete or dirt surfaces during the course of a full marathon, you would be wise to do a good portion of your training on those same surfaces. But, in the case of the marathon, that may not be true. There has been very little scientific research done concerning the differences between training for the marathon on the treadmill versus free range training, so we are limited to using the small amount of data we have to make a decision.

I mentioned in an earlier chapter (page 86) that I completed a personal experiment in which I did nearly all of my marathon training runs on the treadmill. The result was somewhat surprising to me in that I ran very close to my course PR. There are also documented accounts of elite marathon runners that also performed all or most of their training runs on the treadmill and finished their goal races in top times.

Why does running so many workouts, including long runs, on the treadmill, not have an adverse effect on performance? There have been few reliable studies done to confidently answer that question, but one possible answer may be the more forgiving surface of the treadmill. The training law of specificity states that your training should match your goal as closely as possible. So, in most cases you should do a good portion of your training on the same surface as your goal race. This is true for shorter races. But, when doing those all important long training runs, you are placing a great deal of repetitive stress on your muscles and tendons. That much stress in training can be the cause of going into the race with muscles and tendons that are damaged and fatigued. Perhaps, doing long runs on the treadmill removes some of that stress and allows you to go into your race with fresher legs. This is just an educated guess on my part, but until conclusive research is done on the subject, educated guesses are all we have to rely upon. The bottom line is that I have seen enough data from myself, runners I coach and even world class runners to convince me that most of your marathon training runs can be completed on the treadmill with very little adverse effect on your performance. That being said, I still also believe that you should follow the rule of specificity and do at least a couple of your long runs and several of your other training runs, outside on the road, trail or track.

Prerequisite:

Before beginning this program you should complete the pre-season build up or have a sufficient base of fitness already in place.

Week 1

Day	Workout	Comments
1	The Big Easy or Rest	Freshman level take the day off, intermediate and expert level do 6 miles
2	The Cruiser	Freshman level do 4 miles, intermediate level do 5 miles, expert level do 6 miles
3	The Big Easy	All levels do 6 miles
4	400 Meter Repeats	Freshman level do 6 repeats, intermediate level do 8 repeats, expert level do 10 repeats
5	The Big Easy	All levels do 6 miles
6	Hill Fartlek	All levels do 3 miles
7	Easy Marathon Run	Freshman level do 12 miles, intermediate level do 13 miles, expert level do 15 miles.

Week 2

Day	Workout	Comments
1	The Big Easy or Rest	Freshman level rest, intermediate and expert level do 6 miles.
2	The Cruiser	Freshman level do 5 miles, intermediate level do 6 miles, expert level do 7 miles
3	The Big Easy	All levels do 6 miles
4	400 Meter Repeats with a Float	Freshman level do 6 repeats, intermediate level do 8 repeats, expert level do 10 repeats
5	The Big Easy	All levels do 6 miles
6	The Foothills	All levels do one workout
7	Easy Marathon Run	Freshman level do 7 miles, intermediate level do 9 miles, expert level do 11 miles

Week 3

Day	Workout	Comments
1	The Big Easy or Rest	Freshman level rest, intermediate and expert level do 6 miles
2	LT Pyramid	Freshman level do 1 pyramid, intermediate and expert level do 2 pyramids
3	The Big Easy	Freshman level do 6 miles, intermediate level do 7 miles, expert level do 8 miles
4	400 Meter Repeats with a Float	Freshman level do 8 repeats, intermediate level do 10 repeats, expert level do 12 repeats
5	The Big Easy	All levels do 6 miles
6	Rolling Hills	All levels do one workout
7	Marathon in the Middle	Freshman level do 12 miles with 2 of those miles in the middle of the run at goal race pace. Intermediate level do 13 miles with 3 of those miles in the middle of the run at goal race pace. Expert level do 14 miles with 4 of those miles in the middle of the run at goal race pace

Week 4

Day	Workout	Comments
1	The Big Easy or Rest	Freshman level rest, intermediate and expert level do 6 miles
2	LT Pyramid	Freshman level do 2 pyramids, intermediate and expert levels do 3 pyramids
3	The Big Easy	Freshman level do 6 miles, intermediate level do 7 miles, expert level do 8 miles
4	800 Meter Repeats	Freshman level do 3 repeats, intermediate level do 4 repeats, expert level do 6 repeats
5	The Big Easy	All levels do 6 miles
6	Hill Fartlek	Freshman level do 3 miles, intermediate level do 4 miles, expert level do 5 miles
7	Easy Marathon Run	Freshman level do 9 miles, intermediate level do 11 miles, expert level do 13 miles

Week 5

Day	Workout	Comments
1	The Big Easy or Rest	Freshman level take the day off, intermediate and expert level do 6 miles
2	The Miracle Miles	All levels do one workout
3	The Big Easy	Freshman level do 7 miles, intermediate level do 8 miles, expert level do 9 miles
4	800 Meter Repeats Increasing Pace	Freshman level do 3 repeats, intermediate level do 4 repeats, expert level do 6 repeats
5	The Big Easy	All levels do 6 miles
6	The Foothills	All levels do one workout
7	Marathon Mimic	Freshman level do 14 miles with 11 at an easy pace followed by 3 at goal race pace. Intermediate level do 15 miles with 10 miles at an easy pace and 5 at goal race pace. Expert level do 16 miles with 9 miles at an easy pace followed by 7 at goal race pace

Week 6

Day	Workout	Comments
1	The Big Easy or Rest	Freshman level rest, intermediate and expert level do 6 miles
2	LT Superset	Freshman level do 1 superset, intermediate level do 2 supersets, expert level do 3 supersets.
3	The Big Easy	Freshman level do 7 miles, intermediate level do 8 miles, expert level do 10 miles
4	800 Meter Repeats Increasing Pace	Freshman level do 3 repeats, intermediate level do 5 repeats, expert level do 7 repeats
5	The Big Easy	All levels do 6 miles
6	Hill Progression	All levels do one workout
7	Easy Marathon Run	Freshman level do 11 miles, intermediate level do 13 miles, expert level do 15 miles

Week 7

Day	Workout	Comments
1	The Big Easy or Rest	Freshman level rest, intermediate and expert level do 6 miles
2	LT Superset	Freshman level do 2 supersets, intermediate level do 3 supersets, expert level do 4 supersets
3	The Big Easy	Freshman level do 7 miles, intermediated level do 8 miles, expert level do 10 miles
4	800 Meter Repeats Increasing Pace	Freshman level do 4 repeats, intermediate level do 6 repeats, expert level do 8 repeats
5	The Big Easy	All levels do 6 miles
6	Hill Fartlek	Freshman level do 3 miles, intermediate level do 4 miles, expert level do 5 miles
7	Marathon Mimic	Freshman level do 16 miles with 12 at an easy pace followed by 4 at goal race pace. Intermediate level do 17 miles with 11 miles at an easy pace and 6 at goal race pace. Expert level do 18 miles with 10 miles at an easy pace and 8 at goal race pace

Week 8

Day	Workout	Comments
1	Rest	All levels rest
2	2 Mile Repeats	Freshman level do 3 repeats, intermediate and expert level do 4 repeats
3	The Big Easy	Freshman level do 6 miles, intermediate level do 7 miles, expert level do 8 miles
4	Speed Pyramid	All levels do one workout
5	Rest	All levels rest
6	Hill Blasters	All levels do one workout
7	Easy Marathon Run	Freshman level do 13 miles, intermediate level do 15 miles, expert level do 17 miles

Week 9

Day	Workout	Comments
1	The Big Easy or Rest	Freshman level rest, intermediate and expert level do 6 miles
2	20 Minute Repeats	All levels do 2 repeats
3	The Big Easy	Freshman level do 7 miles, intermediate level do 8 miles, expert level do 10 miles
4	3 x 1 Mile Repeats	All levels do one workout
5	The Big Easy	All levels do 6 miles
6	The Hill Climb	Freshman level do 2 miles, intermediate level do 3 miles, expert level do 5 miles
7	Marathon Mimic	Freshman level do 18 miles with 12 at an easy pace followed by 6 at goal race pace. Intermediate level do 19 miles with 11 at an easy pace followed by 8 at goal race pace. Expert level do 20 miles with 10 miles at an easy pace followed by 10 at goal race pace

Week 10

Day	Workout	Comments
1	Rest	All levels rest
2	The Cruiser	Freshman level do 6 miles, intermediate level do 7 miles, expert level do 8 miles
3	The Big Easy	Freshman level do 6 miles, intermediate level do 7 miles, expert level do 8 miles
4	5 x 3 Minute Repeats	All levels do one workout
5	The Big Easy	All levels do 6 miles
6	Rolling Hills	All levels do one workout
7	Easy Marathon Run	Freshman level do 15 miles, intermediate level do 17 miles, expert level do 19 miles

Week 11

Day	Workout	Comments
1	The Big Easy or Rest	Freshman level rest, intermediate and expert level do 6 miles
2	5K Repeats	All levels do 2 repeats
3	The Big Easy	Freshman level do 7 miles, intermediate level do 8 miles, expert level do 10 miles
4	3 x 1 Mile Repeats	All levels do one workout
5	The Big Easy	All levels do 6 miles
6	The Hill Climb	Freshman level do 3 miles, intermediate level do 5 miles, expert level do 7 miles
7	Marathon Mimic With a Kick	Freshman level do 20 miles with 12 at an easy pace followed by 7 at goal race pace and 1 at 10K pace. Intermediate level do 21 miles with 11 at an easy pace followed by 9 at goal race pace and 1 at 10K pace. Expert level do 22 miles with 10 miles at an easy pace, at goal race pace followed by 10 at goal race pace and 2 at 10K pace

Week 12

Day	Workout	Comments
1	Rest	All levels rest
2	Marathon Madness	Freshman level do 6 miles, intermediate level do 8 miles, expert level do 10 miles
3	The Big Easy	Freshman level do 6 miles, intermediate level do 7 miles, expert level do 8 miles
4	Speed Pyramid	All levels do one workout
5	Rest	All levels rest
6	Pike's Peak	All levels do one workout
7	Easy Marathon Run	Freshman level do 17 miles, intermediate level do 18 miles, expert level do 20 miles

Week 13

Day	Workout	Comments
1	The Big Easy or Rest	Freshman level rest, intermediate and expert levels do 6 miles
2	5K Repeats	All levels do 2 repeats
3	The Big Easy	Freshman level do 7 miles, intermediate level do 8 miles, expert level do 10 miles
4	5 x 3 Minute Repeats	All levels do one workout
5	The Big Easy	All levels do 6 miles
6	The Hill Climb	Freshman level do 4 miles, intermediate level do 6 miles, expert level do 8 miles
7	Marathon Mimic With a Kick	Freshman level do 22 miles with 12 at an easy pace, followed by 9 at goal race pace and 1 at 10K pace. Intermediate level do 23 miles with 12 at an easy pace followed by 9 at goal race pace and 2 miles at 10K pace. Expert level do 24 miles with 12 at an easy pace and 9 at goal race pace and 3 at 10K pace

Week 14

Day	Workout	Comments
1	Rest	All levels rest
2	Two Mile Repeats	Freshman level do 3 repeats, intermediate and expert level do 4 repeats
3	The Big Easy	Freshman level do 6 miles, intermediate level do 7 miles, expert level do 8 miles
4	800 Meter Repeats Increasing Pace	Freshman level do 6 repeats, intermediate level do 8 repeats, expert level do 10 repeats
5	The Big Easy	Freshman level do 6 miles, intermediate and expert level do 8 miles
6	Hill Fartlek	All levels do one workout
7	Easy Marathon Run	Freshman level do 10 miles, intermediate level do 12 miles, expert level do 14 miles

Week 15

Day	Workout	Comments
1	The Big Easy or Rest	Freshman level rest, intermediate and expert level do 6 miles
2	One Mile Repeats	Freshman level do 5 repeats, intermediate level do 6 repeats, expert level do 7 repeats
3	The Big Easy	All levels do 6 miles
4	800 Meter Repeats Increasing Pace	Freshman level do 4 repeats, intermediate level do 6 repeats, expert level do 8 repeats
5	The Big Easy	All levels do 6 miles
6	The Hill Climb	All levels do 3 miles
7	Easy Marathon Run	All levels do 10 miles

Week 16

Day	Workout	Comments
1	The Big Easy or Rest	Freshman level take the day off, intermediate and expert levels do 4 miles
2	The Cruiser	All levels do 5 miles
3	The Big Easy	All levels do 6 miles
4	The Big Easy	All levels do 5 miles
5	Rest	All levels rest
6	Rest	All levels rest
7	Race	Race Day

9

Endurance Workouts

The first workouts performed by all runners are en-durance runs. These continuous moderate to long distance runs form the foundation of fitness that every training program is built upon. Endurance workouts are used for aerobic conditioning.

Aerobic conditioning serves a number of purposes.

• It increases the number of mitochondria in the working muscles. Mitochondria are tiny structures in your muscle cells, where all energy production takes place. An increase in the number of mitochondria translates to the ability to produce more energy for running.
• It increases the density of the capillaries in the mus-cles. This means there will be more blood flow and oxygen delivery to your working muscles.
• It improves joint, tendon and ligament strength. Most running injuries are joint and connective tissue re-lated. Stronger connective tissues means less incidence of injury.

• Develops the slow twitch muscle fibers in your legs. Muscle fibers are either slow twitch or fast twitch. The slow twitch fibers are slower to fatigue and are the primary muscle fibers used in distance running.

• Aerobic conditioning increase your blood volume. This enables more oxygen to be delivered to your working muscles.

Aerobic conditioning workouts make up the greatest percentage of all runners training programs, but they are particularly important to beginning runners because they strengthen the connective tissues, which is where most running injuries occur. Most beginning runner's programs are entirely composed of this type of workout. Experienced runners perform these workouts throughout their training season, but they make up a larger portion of the early season workouts when rebuilding from rest periods or injury.

Aerobic conditioning workouts are also known as base training, easy runs and conversational runs. There are actually two different types of aerobic conditioning runs - Recovery runs and easy runs. All recovery runs are easy runs, but not all easy runs are recovery runs.

• Recovery runs - This type of workout is used to recover from an extremely hard workout or race. After a maximal effort your muscles and joints need a period of recovery to restore themselves to a state in which you can resume proper training. Without the recovery time, the muscles and joints do not get a chance to strengthen. This can result in decreased performance and overtraining problems. The amount of recovery needed depends upon the length of the race or workout. As a rule of thumb, one day of recovery is needed for each hard mile run. So, if you are recovering from a marathon, you will need just over three weeks of recovery time before you begin intense training. Recovery runs are also used when rehabilitating an injury. Recovery from an injury may require very easy running or even walking or cross training, while general recovery from a hard workout may be done at a variety of paces.

• Easy runs - Easy runs are performed at a pace between 45 seconds per mile slower than marathon pace and just over marathon pace. The majority of all runners training runs are this type of workout. The purpose of easy runs, as discussed above, are to improve the ability of your muscles to produce energy, increase the blood delivery to the muscles, strengthen the joints and burn calories to maintain an ideal body weight.

The Big Easy

This is a basic easy run. The distance of this run may be anywhere between 10 and 12 miles. If you are a new runner, keep the distance between 2 and 6 miles. A more experienced runner could run up to 12 miles. Running further than 12 miles will add unnecessary physical stress and will defeat the purpose of an easy run. Runs of longer than 12 miles become a long run, which has a different purpose and goal.

This is a very versatile workout that can be used for many purposes, including improving your endurance, building a base of fitness, burning calories and recovering from a hard workout or race. This workout will make up the majority of a beginner's training schedule.

To add some variety, you could vary the pace during your run. Just keep the pace between one minute per mile slower than your current marathon pace and 15 seconds slower than marathon pace. If you do not know your marathon pace, run at a pace that is "conversational". You should be able to speak and carry on a conversation, but you should not be able to sing. If you cannot speak clearly, you are running too fast. If you can sing, you are running to slowly.

In most cases, heart rate levels should be around 75% of maximum for this workout. Heart rate levels will fluctuate during all training runs. It is especially common for heart rates to rise during the later stages of a training run. This workout will probably follow that pattern, so do not be surprised to see your heart rate rise to 80% or even a bit higher.

Time/Distance	Pace	Elevation
10 Minutes	Warm Up	1%
2 to 12 Miles	Easy - 1 Minute to 15 Seconds Slower than Marathon Pace	1%

The Freshman Starter

Before you learned to walk you had to crawl. Learning to run is the same. If you are new to running, you must start with walking and gradually add in some short, easy running segments.

Your first workout should be 30 minutes of walking. Your next workout should also be 30 minutes, but alternate between 5 minutes of walking and 15 seconds of easy running. For each successive 30 minute workout, add 15 seconds of running until you are walking 5 minutes and running 5 minutes. Then start decreasing your walking segment by 15 seconds in each workout. For example, after a workout composed of alternating 5 minutes of running with 5 minutes of walking, your next workout would be alternating 4 minutes and 45 seconds of walking alternating with 5 minutes of easy running. Keep up this sequence until you are running the entire 30 minute workout.

Time/Distance	Pace	Elevation
30 Minutes	Alternating between walking at a brisk pace and running at an easy pace	1%

The Junk Eliminator

I started to run competitively in the early 1970's. During those days, many runner's training programs were judged by how many miles they had in their training logs. It became of a contest of "keeping up with the Jones'. If your running partner did 100 miles last week, then you wanted to run 110 miles to top him. Most of those miles were built up with long, easy runs. As we already discussed, this type of run does provide aerobic benefits. Running more mileage usually translates to higher levels of fitness and better running performance, up to a point. The problem lies in why the mileage is being performed. Many runners put in a lot of easy miles that serve no defined purpose other than padding that mileage total in their running log. This type of mileage is known as "junk miles". Junk miles should be avoided because they do very little in terms of fitness gains, and add unnecessary stress to your muscles and joints.

Junk mileage becomes a problem when you just run with no purpose or goal in mind. You should always have a reason for doing your workout. In the case of easy runs, your goal may be aerobic conditioning, recovery or calorie burn. This workout is designed to make a run that could be considered junk miles a more quality workout.

The total mileage for this run can be anywhere from 3 miles to 10 miles. Run at an easy pace. This workout is like every other easy run, except that you will increase your speed to 10K pace or about 90% of your maximum heart rate for 30 seconds out of every 5 minutes. This will add some quality pace running to your workout, but not enough fast running to offset the rest and recovery that you need during your easy runs.

Time/Distance	Pace	Elevation
10 Minutes	Warm Up	1%
3 to 10 Miles	5 minutes easy alternating with 30 seconds at 10K pace	1%

The Aerobic Circuit

This is a cross training workout that combines an easy run with another form of cardiovascular exercise. Cross training works muscles and tendons that you do not use or use to a lesser extent when running.

To perform this workout you will need another form of cardiovascular exercise in addition to your treadmill. The other exercise can be an exercise bike, stair stepper, elliptical machine or even a jump rope or a raised step. Any type of exercise, other than running, that is cardiovascular in nature and will raise your heart rate to 70% of maximum, will work.

After a warm up, exercise for 30 minutes alternating between 3 minutes on your treadmill and 2 minutes on your cross training exercise. Do not allow yourself to cool off between the alternating exercises. Go from one exercise to the next with no rest. Try to perform the cross training exercise at the same intensity level that you are doing the running portions of the workout.

Time	Pace	Exercise
10 Minutes	Warm Up	Treadmill
3 Minutes	Easy	Treadmill
2 Minutes	Easy	Cross Train
3 Minutes	Easy	Treadmill
2 Minutes	Easy	Cross Train
3 Minutes	Easy	Treadmill
2 Minutes	Easy	Cross Train
3 Minutes	Easy	Treadmill
2 Minutes	Easy	Cross Train
3 Minutes	Easy	Treadmill
2 Minutes	Easy	Cross Train
3 Minutes	Easy	Treadmill
2 Minutes	Easy	Cross Train

The Strength Circuit

Strength training is an important part of training that is ignored by many runners. Running speed and endurance depends, a great deal, on the amount of power that your legs can generate with the least amount of effort. Before you can develop that power, you must build strength. This workout combines the benefits of an easy run with some general strength training exercises that will begin to build a base of strength that you can improve and develop.

This workout is considered an endurance workout because of the low intensity of the running portions, but it is not an easy workout. You will move between the running portions and the strength portions with no rest.

After a warm up, exercise for 35 minutes alternating between easy running and a strength training exercise, using the following routine or a similar routine:

Time	Pace/Exercise	Elevation
5 Minutes	Easy Running	1%
30 Seconds	Push Ups	
5 Minutes	Easy Running	1%
30 Seconds	One Leg Squats	
5 Minutes	Easy Running	1%
30 Seconds	Triceps Press Ups	
5 Minutes	Easy Running	1%
30 Seconds	Abdominal Crunches	
5 Minutes	Easy Running	1%
30 Seconds	Bench Step Ups	
5 Minutes	Easy Running	1%
30 Seconds	Biceps Curls	
5 Minutes	Easy Running	1%

Descriptions of these strength training exercises are listed on the following pages.

• Push ups - Begin face down on the floor, supporting yourself with your hands approximately shoulder width apart and your arms extended. Your feet can be together or up to 12 inches apart. Keep your body in a straight and neutral position. Do not arch your back. Contract your abdominal muscles to stabilize your spine. Slowly lower your upper body until your chest touches or nearly touches the

floor. Slowly return to the starting position. If you are unable to perform this type of push up, do bent knee push-ups, which are the same as the regular pushup, except you are supporting your lower body on your knees instead of your feet.

• One Leg Squats - Stand in an upright position. Contract your abdominal muscles to stabilize your trunk and spine. Place one foot (rear foot) behind you on a bench or step that is 6 to 18 inches high. Your other foot (forward foot) should be flat on the floor and directly under your center of gravity. Bend your forward knee until it is at approximately a 90-degree angle. Do not allow your knee to extend in front of your foot. Slowly straighten your forward leg and

return to the starting position. Repeat this exercise switching leg positions.

• Triceps press ups - Sit with your back to a bench or step of approximately 18 inches. Place your hands flat on the bench behind you with your elbows pointing directly behind you. Slowly press yourself up until your arms are fully extended. Slowly return to the starting position.

• Abdominal crunches - Lie face up on an exercise ball. Keep you feet flat on the floor. Cross your hands over your chest and tuck your chin into your chest. Slowly curl your upper body towards your knees. This should be a rolling, curling motion. Concentrate on strongly contracting your abdominal muscles. Hold this position for a moment and slowly return to the starting position.

• Bench step ups - Stand in an upright position. Contract your abdominal muscles to stabilize your trunk and spine. Stand directly in front of a bench that is 18 to 24 inches high. Place one foot (lead foot) flat on the bench. With most of your weight on the heel of your lead foot, forcefully push off with your lead foot and assume a standing position with both feet on the bench. Switch leg position and repeat.

• Biceps curls - Stand upright holding a light weight in each hand with your palms facing forward, away from your body. Contract your abdominal muscles to stabilize your trunk and spine. Keep your upper arms against your ribs and perpendicular to the floor. Slowly raise the weight by flexing your arms at your elbows. Keep your upper arms stationary. Raise the weight to the limit of your active and natural motion. Slowly return to the starting position.

The Day After

The day after running a marathon, most of us regress into a slow, stumbling and unsteady walk that is affectionately known as the "marathon shuffle". This muscle soreness and stiffness is caused by the trauma that 26.2 hard miles can inflict on our body. Some TLC is needed to help soothe our overworked muscles. That is what this workout is designed to do. While we feel like just lying in bed and not moving, a little "hair of the dog that bit you" will actually do you more good. Some light exercise and stretching will assist in the repair and recovery of your sore muscles.

This is strictly a recovery workout that should be performed for anywhere from a few days to a week following a marathon. You do not have to do a marathon in order do this workout. This training run could be used following any hard race or workout, when you feel sore and fatigued.

Start the workout with 5 minutes of walking. After about 5 minutes your muscles should start to feel a bit less stiff. If you still feel extremely stiff, walk for an additional 5 minutes. Then break into a very easy jog for about 5 minutes. Continue to alternate 5 minutes of walking with 5 minutes of easy jogging. After finishing your workout, do some very light stretching. A nice soak in a hot tub will feel great after this workout.

Continue doing this workout daily until your muscle soreness is gone and your legs no longer feel like dead weights.

Time	Pace	Elevation
5 Minutes	Warm Up	1%
5 Minutes	Easy Jog	1%
5 Minutes	Walk	1%
5 Minutes	Easy Jog	1%
5 Minutes	Walk	1%
5 Minutes	Easy Jog	1%
5 Minutes	Walk	1%

The Fat Buster

Weight loss is one of the reasons that many beginning runners decide to take up the sport. They do this for good reason. Treadmill running burns more calories per hour than any other type of exercise machine. Weight loss is a function of calories in versus calories out. If you burn more calories than you take in, on a daily basis, you will lose weight. I am sure that you have read at various times, that if you want to lose weight, you should exercise in the "weight loss zone". No, that is not a black and white horror series narrated by Rod Serling. The "Zone" is an exercise heart rate range of approximately 65% to 75% that is touted by some to be the ideal exercise intensity for weight loss. They tell you that if you exercise at a higher intensity, you are not burning fat. They are partially right, but mostly wrong.

When you are exercising at a low intensity, you are exercising aerobically, which means "with oxygen". When you are exercising aerobically, you are burning both fat and carbohydrates to produce energy. In contrast, when you are exercising as hard as you can, such as when you are sprinting, your body cannot use oxygen fast enough to provide enough energy. At this point you are exercising anaerobically, which means "without oxygen." When you are exercising anaerobically you are burning mostly carbohydrates to produce the energy. The proponents of the "Zone" system do not want you to stray above the fat burning zone because they feel that the goal is to burn as much fat as possible during your workout. That sounds good in theory, but in practice it is the wrong approach. You actually burn very little fat in any one workout. For weight loss, your goal should be to maximize your calorie burn in every workout. To do this you need to include some intense exercise in your run. Why? - Because higher intensity exercise does two important things for you:

- It burns more calories per minute than low intensity exercise.
- It improves your level of fitness and makes improvements in your body at the cellular level that trains you to improve the pace of your easy runs so that you begin to burn even more calories in all of your workouts. It improves your body's ability to burn fat as fuel.

This workout is designed to increase the calories burned during your run, while maintaining the overall easy qualities of the workout. In this workout you will run for 30 minutes alternating between 5 minutes at an easy pace and short 1 minute repeats at a progressively faster pace.

Time	Pace	Elevation
5 Minutes	Warm Up	1%
5 Minutes	Easy	1%
1 Minute	Easy plus 15 seconds per mile	1%
5 Minutes	Easy	1%
1 Minute	Easy plus 30 seconds per mile	1%
5 Minutes	Easy	1%
1 Minute	Easy plus 45 seconds per mile	1%
5 Minutes	Easy	1%
1 Minute	Easy plus 1 minute per mile	1%
5 Minutes	Easy	1%
1 Minute	Easy plus 1:15 per mile	1%
5 Minutes	Cool down	1%

The Enforcer

The purpose of recovery runs are to give your muscles and joints the time to repair and rest between hard workouts or after a hard race. The ideal heart rate for recovery is between 65% and 70%. It can be very difficult to force yourself to run this slow. This workout will force you to run at an appropriate recovery pace.

You will need a heart rate monitor to perform this workout. The ideal situation would be to have a treadmill that can be automatically controlled by your heart rate. If you are fortunate enough to have that type of machine, this workout is perfect for you. If you do not have that type of treadmill, you can still do this workout, but will have to monitor your heart rate and make adjustments manually.

This workout is really simple. If your treadmill can be controlled by your heart rate, just enter your minimum heart rate as 65% of your maximum and your maximum heart rate as 70% of your maximum. If you do not know your maximum heart rate (MHR), you can estimate it with the formula of 220 minus your age. So, if you are 40 years old your estimated maximum heart rate is 220 - 40 = 180. Multiply your MHR by 60% to determine your minimum heart rate for this workout. 180 x 60% = 108. In this same example, the maximum heart rate for the workout is determined by multiplying 180 x 70% = 126. Your treadmill will take it from here. If your heart rate strays above the maximum you set, it will either slow down or decrease the elevation until you drop down below that ceiling you set. It becomes your enforcer and keeps you from running too fast. It will also speed up or increase the elevation if you drop below the minimum you set.

If you are using a manual heart rate monitor, you follow the same procedure in determining your minimum and maximum heart rates and make your speed adjustments manually.

Time/Distance	Pace	Elevation
30 Minutes	One to two minutes slower than marathon pace	1%

The Wanderer

Do you have a free spirit? If so, this treadmill endurance workout is for you. This treadmill training run is basically an easy fartlek workout. Fartlek is a funny word used by runners that basically means "speed play". It's often a harder speed workout in which you change your pace frequently throughout your run. There is no real structure to a fartlek run - you change pace at will.

In this workout you will run for between 20 and 60 minutes at paces that vary from an easy pace to a hard pace. You choose the distance, your paces and the treadmill elevation. The only rules here are that you should change them frequently and have fun with this one.

Even thought this is a fun fartlek workout it is also an endurance workout, so keep running throughout the training run. Don't take any breaks for physical or mental recovery. If you are beginning to fatigue physically during this workout either decrease your pace or elevation for some active recovery.

If you've done fartlek runs in the past you're probably used including some very hard running portions. This workout is an endurance version of fartlek running. Do most of your running in this workout at easy to moderate paces. It's OK to include some short, high intensity runs, but keep them short to maintain the endurance aspects of this workout.

Time/Distance	Pace	Elevation
20 to 60 Minutes	Vary your pace at will between an easy pace and a hard pace	Vary your elevation at will between 1% and 5%

The Traveler

I've always envied the athletes that have the time and money to go on long cross country runs. Try as I might I have never been able to come up with the month or more of spare time to do a run like that. Would you like to do a cross country or cross state run? Well - maybe you can. If you can't do the actual run you can do a virtual cross country run on your treadmill. All you need is your treadmill and a large map of the area you want to run across.

This is a fun and motivating endurance run that will get you to your cross country destination from the comfort of your own home. Attach the destination map on a wall near your treadmill. After every run you do move a location pin along the route on your map. If you do a 6 mile run, move your pin 6 miles along the route on your map. That will give you a visual of where you are on your route.

If you know the elevation changes along your route you may want to match your treadmill incline to the incline of your actual route.

There are also a number of websites where you can map your route. If you use one of those site to map your route I would still suggest also using a paper map. The visual reference near your treadmill offers a lot of motivation.

Time/Distance	Pace	Elevation
Any distance. You should run for distance instead of time for this one so you can track your progress	Easy Endurance Pace or 70% to 80% of your maximum heart rate	1% or match the incline of your actual route

The Endurance Duathlon

This is a treadmill workout for all of you multi-sport athletes out there. To perform this workout you will need a stationary or exercise bike as well as your treadmill. During this workout you will perform three stages. The first stage will be a 5K run. Then you will do 10K on your exercise bike followed by another 5K.

You can adjust the distances in this workout to suit your goal and fitness level. For example you could do a 1 mile run, a 5 mile bike and another 1 mile run. If you prefer longer distances you could do a 10K run, a 20K bike and another 10K run.

This is an endurance duathlon workout so keep your pace at easy endurance pace. About 1 to 2 minutes slower than marathon pace or around 70% to 80% of your maximum heart rate.

Time/Distance	Pace	Elevation
5K Run	Easy Endurance Pace	1%
10K Bike	Easy Endurance Pace	N/A
5K Run	Easy Endurance Pace	1%

The Half Marathon Challenge

This is an advanced endurance workout that is an excellent marathon training run. In this training run you will run for 13.1 miles alternating between an easy pace and your goal marathon pace. As you become fitter you can increase the amount of time you spend at marathon pace in this workout, eventually building up to a full half marathon at marathon pace.

If you don't know your marathon pace you can run using either perceived exertion or heart rate. Your marathon pace should be a moderate to moderately hard pace or around 75% to 80% of your maximum heart rate.

Time/Distance	Pace	Elevation
2 miles	Easy Pace	1%
1 mile	Marathon Pace	1%
2 miles	Easy Pace	1%
1 mile	Marathon Pace	1%
1 mile	Easy Pace	1%
1 mile	Marathon Pace	1%
1 mile	Easy Pace	1%
2 miles	Marathon Pace	1%
1 mile	Easy Pace	1%
1.1 mile	Marathon Pace	1%

10

Speed Endurance Workouts

S peed endurance runs have many aliases. They have been called lactate threshold runs, anaerobic conditioning, tempo runs, anaerobic threshold training, sustained runs and steady-state runs. Regardless of what term you use, the goal of these workouts are the same. They are designed to improve the ability of your body to process and produce energy from the lactic acid produced by your running, which will improve your ability to maintain a quality pace over a long distance. The intended pace is from just below to just over your lactate threshold level.

So, what exactly is your lactate threshold level? An in depth discussion of lactate threshold could fill this entire book. The condensed version is that your lactate threshold is the somewhat vague point at which your body starts to produce more lactic acid that it can process. Lactic acid is a by-product of the energy producing process that takes place in your muscles. There are a number of complex process that lead to the accumulation of lactic acid, but I will spare you the gory details. The important fact is that as your running intensity increases, so does your production of lactic acid. When you're running at an easy or moderate pace, your muscles are able to convert the lactic acid to energy. If you continue to run faster, you will reach a point at which the lactic acid is accumulating faster than your muscles can process it. A number of terms have been used to describe this point, including: lactate threshold, anaerobic threshold and ventilatory threshold. Most athletes reach this point at just below their 10K race pace. Once you stray above your lactate threshold, the excess accumulation of lactic acid leads to a increase in the acidity of your bloodstream. This rise in acidity is something that your body does not like. In protest, your body inhibits the activity of enzymes that are required for energy production. The result is that you will eventually be forced to slow down.

Since your lactate threshold has a major influence on your sustainable running speed, it is clear that improving your lactate threshold will also improve your speed endurance and race performance. That is what these lactate threshold workouts are designed to do. When performing these workouts, you will be running at paces that vary from just below to just over your lactate threshold. These paces will train your body to be more efficient at dealing with and processing the lactic acid that is produced.

The following workouts use paces that range from 20 seconds per mile slower than your current 10K race pace to 5K pace. If you do not know what your race pace is, there are two alternatives. You can use either a heart rate monitor or a rating of perceived exertion.

When using a heart rate monitor, your 10K race pace will fall somewhere between 80% and 90% of your maximum heart rate(MHR). Most runners that train using a heart rate monitor will use 85% of their maximum as the goal heart rate.

The rating of perceived exertion uses your perception of how difficult you feel the workout is. A lactic threshold workout should feel difficult, but not quite maximum effort. It should be an effort level that you feel you can maintain for at least 30 minutes without stopping.

The Cruiser

This is a basic workout in which the goal is to maintain a pace that is just below your lactate threshold. Similar workouts have been called cruise intervals, steady-state running and anaerobic threshold runs. This is a key training run that is used for all long distance race training and trains your body to maintain a quality pace for an extended period. This workout also toughens you mentally so that you can keep up a good tempo when fatigued.

After a 5 minute warm up, run between 2 and 10 miles at a pace that is about 15 seconds per mile slower than your current 10K race pace or about 30 seconds slower than your 5K race pace. Perform this workout without stopping or slowing for recovery. The idea is to maintain your pace for the entire duration of the workout. Cool down with 5 minutes of easy running.

Time/Distance	Pace	Elevation
10 Minutes	Warm Up	1%
2 to 10 Miles	About 15 seconds per mile slower than 10K pace or around 80% of your MHR	1%
10 Minutes	Cool Down	1%

Two Mile Repeats

A popular track workout that is easily adapted to the treadmill are two mile repeats. These repeats are done at your current 10K race pace or about 15 seconds per mile slower than your current 5K race pace. That pace is roughly equal to 85% to 90% of your maximum heart rate.

After a warm up, run 2 miles at 10K pace. Then slow down to an easy pace for 1/2 mile to recover. Run the two miles without stopping or slowing down. If you are a beginning runner, start with only one repeat and cool down. If you are an intermediate or advanced runner, complete one or two more repeats. After you complete the first two miles, slow down to an easy pace for 1/2 mile to recover. Repeat this one or two more times. The total distance of this workout is between 2 and 8 miles, depending upon the number of repeats with 2 to 6 miles being executed at 10K race pace.

Time/Elevation	Pace	Elevation
10 Minutes	Warm Up	1%
2 Miles	10K Pace	1%
1/2 Mile	Easy Pace	1%
2 Miles	10K Pace	1%
1/2 Mile	Easy Pace	1%
2 Miles	10K Pace	1%
10 Minutes	Cool Down	1%

5K Repeats

After a warm up, run 5 kilometers (3.1 miles) at your current 10K race pace or about 15 seconds per mile slower than your current 5K race pace (85% to 90% of MHR). In the early stages of your training, do only one repeat and cool down with 1/2 mile of easy running. In later phases of your training, or if you are an advanced runner, do two 5K repeats with 1/2 mile of easy running between the repeats for recovery.

This workout is very good for preparing for a 10K race, but is also used for both shorter and longer distance training.

Time/Distance	Pace	Elevation
10 Minutes	Warm Up	1%
5K	10K Pace	1%
1/2 Mile	Easy Pace	1%
5K	10K Pace	1%
10 Minutes	Cool Down	1%

Marathon Madness

This is a strenuous workout that can be used when training for any distance from a 5K to the marathon. After a warm up, run anywhere between 6 and 10 miles, alternating between 1/2 mile at marathon pace (75% of MHR) and 1/4 mile at 5K pace (95% of MHR). There is no recovery between the 1/2 mile - marathon pace runs and the 1/4 mile - 5K pace surges. This difficult training run works by flooding your body with lactic acid during the 5K surges and then forcing your body to clear and process the accumulated lactic acid during the marathon pace runs. Cool down after this workout with 1 mile of easy running.

Time/Distance	Pace	Elevation
10 Minutes	Warm Up	1%
6 to 10 Miles	Alternate between 1/2 mile at marathon pace and 1/4 mile at 5K pace	1%
10 Minutes	Cool Down	1%

One Mile Repeats

One mile repeats are another popular track workout that is easily accomplished on the treadmill. After a warm up, run one mile at your current 10K race pace (85% to 90 % of MHR) or about 15 second per mile slower than your 5K race pace. Then slow down to an easy pace for 1/4 to 1/2 mile to recover before speeding up again to 10K pace for the next segment. Repeat this 3 to 8 times depending upon your experience and fitness level. This workout can be done progressively over the course of your training cycle. Start with 3 or 4 repeats with 1/2 mile of recovery and gradually progress to 8 repeats with 1/4 mile of recovery in the later stages of your training cycle.

Time/Distance	Pace	Elevation
10 Minutes	Warm Up	1%
1 Mile	10K Pace	1%
1/4 to 1/2 Mile	Easy Pace	1%
1 Mile	10K Pace	1%
1/4 to 1/2 Mile	Easy Pace	1%
1 Mile	10K Pace	1%
1/4 to 1/2 Mile	Easy Pace	1%
1 Mile	10K Pace	1%
1/4 to 1/2 Mile	Easy Pace	1%

Repeat this pattern for your desired number of repetitions. Cool down at the end of your workout with 10 minutes of easy running.

20 Minute Repeats

This is a simple workout that can be done at any time of the year. It is also appropriate for all levels of runners from a beginner to more advanced runners. A beginning runner will want to do only one repeat while intermediate and advanced runner could do two or three repeats. This training run can be done progressively by doing one repeat early in the training cycle and advancing to three repeats at the end of the cycle.

After a warm up, run 20 minutes at your current 10K race pace (85% of MHR) or about 15 seconds per mile slower than your current 5K race pace. Cool down with one mile at an easy pace. If you are doing multiple repeats, recover with 5 minutes of easy running between the repeats.

Time/Distance	Pace	Elevation
10 Minutes	Warm Up	1%
20 Minutes	10K Pace	1%
5 Minutes	Easy Pace	1%
20 Minutes	10K Pace	1%
5 Minutes	Easy Pace	1%

Repeat this pattern for your desired number of repetitions. Cool down at the end of your workout with 10 minutes of easy running.

LT Ladder

A ladder is a workout in which you start with a specific distance run and work progressively up in distance (up the ladder) or down in distance (down the ladder). There are many possible combinations. An example would be: after a warm up, run 1/2 mile at current 10K pace (85% of MHR), then recover with 1/4 mile at an easy pace. Increase your speed again to 10K pace and run 3/4 mile. Recover with 1/4 mile at an easy pace and then return to 10K pace for 1 mile. Finish with a cool down of 1/2 mile at an easy pace. You could reverse this workout by running "down the ladder" by starting with 1 mile followed by 3/4 mile and 1/2 mile. All of the runs being performed at 10K pace with 1/4 mile of easy running in between to recover.

A beginning runner may start with a shorter ladder such as 1/4 mile, 1/2 mile and 3/4 mile. Advanced runners could progress to a much more difficult workout that is comprised of a 1/2 mile, 3/4 mile, 1 mile, 1.5 mile progression.

Time/Distance	Pace	Elevation
10 Minutes	Warm Up	1%
1/2 Mile	10K Pace	1%
1/4 Mile	Easy Pace	1%
3/4 Mile	10K Pace	1%
1/4 Mile	Easy Pace	1%
1 Mile	10K Pace	1%
1/4 Mile	Easy Pace	1%

LT Pyramid

Pyramids are an extension of the ladder workouts. A pyramid training run is a run up the ladder combined with a run down the ladder. An example is: 1/2 mile, 3/4 mile, 1 mile, 3/4 mile, 1/2 mile. All of the runs are performed at around 10K race pace. There is a 1/4 mile recovery run at an easy pace between each hard effort. Generally speaking, a ladder workout is performed early in the training cycle and the pyramids are introduced later in the cycle as your fitness level increases. Just as with the ladder workouts, there are many possible interval combinations that can be used. Since this workout is intended to improve your lactate threshold, the pace should at or just below your current 10K race pace (85% of MHR) or about 15 seconds per mile slower than your current 5K race pace.

Time/Distance	Pace	Elevation
10 Minutes	Warm Up	1%
1/2 Mile	10K Pace	1%
1/4 Mile	Easy Pace	1%
3/4 Mile	10K Pace	1%
1/4 Mile	Easy Pace	1%
1 Mile	10K Pace	1%
1/4 Mile	Easy Pace	1%
3/4 Mile	10K Pace	1%
1/4 Mile	Easy Pace	1%
1/2 Mile	10K Pace	1%

LT Superset

A superset is a set of intervals that vary in both distance and pace. There are no recovery intervals in a superset. You switch between the various distances and speeds with no rest periods. This is a strenuous training run that should be completed no more than once every two week.

There are an almost unlimited number of possible combinations of pace and distance. The purpose of this workout is lactate threshold improvement, so pace should range from marathon pace to 10K pace.

One possible example of this workout is: After a warm up, run 1/2 mile at 10K pace, then slow down to 10 seconds less than 10K pace for 3/4 mile followed by 1 mile at marathon pace. This entire workout is preformed with no recovery intervals or rest. You can also do multiple supersets. An example of this is: After a warm up, run 1/2 mile at 10K pace followed by 3/4 mile at marathon pace. Repeat this 3 times with 1/2 mile of easy running to recover between each superset. You can design you own workout, but keep your paces at between 10K speed and marathon pace. Your supersets should progress from shorter, easier workouts, to longer more difficult workouts as your fitness level increases.

Time/Distance	Pace	Elevation
10 Minutes	Warm Up	1%
1/2 Mile	10K Pace	1%
3/4 Mile	10 seconds per mile slower than 10K pace	1%
1 Mile	Marathon Pace	1%
10 Minutes	Cool Down	1%

The Miracle Miles

This training run is a very popular workout for cross country teams. It combines some 10K pace lactate threshold running with long recovery intervals. This workout can be performed at any time during the year.

After a warm up, run 1 mile at your current 10K race pace. Now slow down to an easy pace for one mile. Then, speed back up to 10K pace for 1 mile. Decrease your speed to an easy pace for another mile and then increase your pace to 10K pace for 1 mile. Slow back down to an easy pace for one more mile and then finish the workout with 1/4 mile at the fastest speed you can maintain for the full 1/4 mile. The all out surge at the end will mimic your kick at the end of the race and improves your ability to run hard when fatigued.

Time/Distance	Pace	Elevation
10 Minutes	Warm Up	1%
1 Mile	10K Pace	1%
1 Mile	Easy Pace	1%
1 Mile	10K Pace	1%
1 Mile	Easy Pace	1%
1 Mile	10K Pace	1%
1 Mile	Easy Pace	1%
1/4 Mile	Fastest speed you can maintain for the 1/4 mile surge	1%
10 Minutes	Cool Down	1%

10K Blaster Superset

This is a form of a superset that is a great workout for 10K training, but can be used for all distances.

After a warm up, run 1/2 mile at 5K pace. Then slow down to 10K pace for the next mile. Now slow further to 20 seconds per mile slower than 10K pace for 3 miles. Next, speed back up to 10K pace for the final 1.5 miles. There is no recovery or rest between the various paces of this workout.

Most runners will only be able to complete one set. Some advanced athletes could to two sets with 10 minutes of recovery between the two sets.

Time/Distance	Pace	Elevation
10 Minutes	Warm Up	1%
1/2 Mile	5K Pace	1%
1 Mile	10K Pace	1%
3 Miles	20 seconds per mile slower than 10K pace	1%
1.5 Miles	10K pace	1%
10 Minutes	Cool Down	1%

10K Ladder

The 6 mile ladder is a simple but moderately difficult workout that is excellent for both lactate threshold and 10K race performance improvement.

Warm up and then run 2 miles at 30 seconds per mile slower than your current 10K pace. With no recovery, speed up to 15 seconds under your current 10K pace for 2 miles. Now, with no recovery, speed up to 10K pace for two more miles. Next, again, with no recovery, speed up to full pace for the final 2/10th miles. Run the last 2/10th miles at the fastest pace you can maintain for the distance.

This workout will not only improve your lactate threshold levels, but will also simulate 10K race conditions and prepare you for the mental and physical challenges of the race.

Time/Distance	Pace	Elevation
10 Minutes	Warm Up	1%
2 Miles	30 seconds per mile slower than 10K pace	1%
2 Miles	15 seconds per mile slower than 10K pace	1%
2 Miles	10K Pace	1%
.2 Miles	Fastest pace you can maintain for the entire 2/10th mile surge	1%
10 Minutes	Cool Down	1%

Progressive Tempo Run

This workout is a variation of the classic tempo run earlier in this chapter called The Cruiser. It's just as simple to perform and is in many ways more enjoyable because your body gradually warms up to tempo pace. You feel stronger through the middle portions of the run and are able to finish at a faster pace. To do a progressive tempo run start with 1 mile at easy endurance pace. Then gradually and evenly increase your pace over the next 2 to 8 miles, so that you are running at your LT or 10K race pace at the end of your run. This type of tempo run give you the additional advantages of running the last mile or so at LT pace and also improving your ability to run faster at the end of a long, quality run.

Time/Distance	Pace	Elevation
1 Mile	Easy Endurance Pace	1%
2 to 8 Miles	Gradually increase your pace from easy endurance pace to your current 10K race pace or about 85% to 90% of your MHR	1%

Race Pace Duathon

Are you ready for a challenge? This workout will give it to you. In the endurance section I have an endurance duathlon workout that is more of a training run. This duathlon workout a race mimic workout. It's as close you can get to doing the real thing without the entry fee.

To do this workout you will need an exercise bike along with your treadmill and a lot of energy.

Start this race mimic workout with a 10 or 15 minute easy warm up jog on your treadmill. Then get ready for the start of your race.

Begin with 5K at your estimated duathlon race pace. Remember that you will be doing two running phases and one bicycling phase without stopping. So you actual race pace for the 5K run segments will probably be closer to your 10K race pace or about 15 to 20 seconds per mile slower than your current 5K race pace.

After the first 5K segment hop on your bike for a 20K bike ride at race intensity before finishing with another 5K run on your treadmill.

Now congratulate yourself for successfully finishing a race pace duathlon. Next step - register for the real thing!

Time/Distance	Pace	Elevation
10 to 15 Minutes	Easy Warm Up Pace	1%
5K	Duathon Race Pace Run	1%
20K	Race Pace Bike Ride	N/A
5K	Duathon Race Pace Run	1%
10 Minutes	Easy Cool Down Run	1%

11

Speed Workouts

There are several different types of workouts that are intended to help improve overall long distance running speed. Speed workouts have been called VO_2 max, vVO_2 max, interval training, speedwork and running economy workouts.

Speed workouts fall into one of two categories:

• Aerobic Capacity Workouts - These workouts are performed at fast paces that are at approximately your current VO_2 max pace. For most runners this will be at between your current 3K and 8K paces. VO_2 max is a measure of the maximum amount of oxygen that can be delivered and used by your working muscles to produce energy. A higher VO_2 max means that you are able to run a faster pace for a longer distance.

• Anaerobic Capacity Workouts - This type of workout is true speedwork and is performed at paces that range from around 3K pace to all out effort. These intense workouts are designed to improve footspeed, short term running speed and strength.

Because of the very fast pace of speed workouts, they are broken up into short repeats with rest intervals inserted between the work repeats. This is the origin of the  term "interval training". The fast pace of these workouts can also place some limitations on the use of the treadmill. The top speed of most treadmills are in the 10 to 12 MPH range, which is 5:00 to 6:00 minutes per mile. This will be fast enough for most runners to perform their speedwork. However, some top runners do their speed work at faster than the typical top treadmill speed of 6:00/mile. If you are one of these fortunate athletes, you will need to do at least some of your speedwork on the track.

400 Meter Repeats

These are short repeats at are performed at just faster than your current 5K pace. This is a standard track interval workout that is easily done on a treadmill. The precision of the treadmill even increases the quality of this type of training run.

After a warm up, run 1/4 mile at just faster than your current 5K race pace. Recover with 1/4 mile at an easy pace. Repeat this 6 to 12 times. Start your training with fewer repeats and gradually build up the number of repeats as your fitness level increases.

Time/Distance	Pace	Elevation
10 Minutes	Warm Up	1%
1/4 Mile	5 to 10 seconds faster than 5K pace	1%
1/4 Mile	Warm Up	1%
1/4 Mile	5 to 10 seconds faster than 5K pace	1%
1/4 Mile	Warm Up	1%
1/4 Mile	5 to 10 seconds faster than 5K pace	1%
1/4 Mile	Warm Up	1%
1/4 Mile	5 to 10 seconds faster than 5K pace	1%

Keep up this pattern for your planned number of repetitions. You should be able to maintain your pace for all of your work repeats. If you find you are no longer able to maintain that pace either increase the time of the recovery interval or decrease the number of repetitions.

400 Meter Repeats with a Float

This workout is very similar to standard 400 meter (1/4 mile) repeats. There are two differences. The 400 meter repeats are performed at 5K pace and the recovery intervals are shorter and faster - 200 meters at a strong but relaxed pace. After a short warm up, run 1/4 mile at your current 5K race pace, then slow down for a 1/8th mile float. The float is not run at an easy pace. The pace should be strong and relaxed. The exact pace will depend upon your particular fitness level. It should be a strong pace, but slow enough so that you can complete this tough workout. If you run your floats too fast, you will not be able to maintain your 5K pace for the entire workout. Your float pace should feel fairly hard, but not maximal. Try doing your first floats at around 20 seconds per mile slower than your current 10K pace. You may need to adjust this pace up or down depending upon your current level of fitness.

Time/Distance	Pace	Elevation
10 Minutes	Warm Up	1%
1/4 Mile	5K pace	1%
1/8 Mile	Float - strong, but relaxed pace.	1%
1/4 Mile	5K pace	1%
1/8 Mile	Float - strong, but relaxed pace	1%
1/4 Mile	5K pace	1%
1/8 Mile	Float - strong, but relaxed pace	1%
1/4 Mile	5K pace	1%
1/8 Mile	Float - strong, but relaxed pace	1%

Continue this pattern for your desired number of repeats. It is important to maintain your planned pace and good form. If either your pace or form begin to deteriorate, stop the workout at that point.

800 Meter Repeats

This is another popular track interval workout that translates very well to the treadmill. After a warm up, run 1/2 mile at your current 5K race pace. Then slow down to an easy pace for 1/4 mile to recover. Repeat this 4 to 8 times. Start with 4 repetitions early in your training and gradually increase to 8 repetitions as your fitness level increases.

Time/Distance	Pace	Elevation
10 Minutes	Warm Up	1%
1/2 Mile	5K Pace	1%
1/4 Mile	Easy Pace	1%
1/2 Mile	5K Pace	1%
1/4 Mile	Easy Pace	1%
1/2 Mile	5K Pace	1%
1/4 Mile	Easy Pace	1%
1/2 Mile	5K Pace	1%
1/4 Mile	Easy Pace	1%

Continue this patter of 1/4 mile at 5K pace followed by 1/4 mile at an easy recovery pace for your desired number of repeats. As with all speed workouts, you should discontinue the workout if your pace or running form begins to deteriorate.

800 Meter Repeats Increasing Pace

This training run is a variation of the standard 800 meter (1/2 mile) repeats. This is a tougher run and does a good job of simulating race conditions in which the pace usually picks up in the last portion of the race.

After a warm up, run 1/2 mile at your current 5K race pace. Slow down to an easy pace for 1/4 mile to recover. Repeat this 4 to 6 times. Each time you repeat this, increase the pace of the 1/2 mile repeat by 2 to 3 seconds per mile. Keep the recovery interval at 1/4 mile with an easy pace.

Time/Distance	Pace	Elevation
10 Minutes	Warm Up	1%
1/2 Mile	5K Pace	1%
1/4 Mile	Easy recovery pace.	1%
1/2 Mile	2 to 3 seconds per mile faster than 5K pace	1%
1/4 Mile	Easy recovery pace	1%
1/2 Mile	5 to 6 seconds per mile faster than 5K pace	1%
1/4 Mile	Easy recovery pace	1%
1/2 Mile	8 to 9 seconds per mile faster than 5K pace	1%
1/4 Mile	Easy recovery pace	1%
1/2 Mile	11 to 12 seconds per mile faster than 5K pace	1%
1/4 Mile	Easy recovery pace	1%
1/2 Mile	14 to 15 seconds per mile faster than 5K pace	1%
1/4 Mile	Easy recovery pace.	1%

3 x 1 Mile Repeats

5K pace is commonly used for repeats of 400 to 1200 meters, but they can also be used for repeats as long as one mile. This is a difficult workout that is very good for developing your ability to handle the intense 5K pace for long distances. This workout is excellent for preparing for the 5K, but is also very useful for improving your ability to run at near VO_2 max pace for long distances.

After a warm up, run one mile at your current 5K race pace. Then slow down to an easy pace for 800 meters to recover. Repeat this 3 times.

As your fitness level increases, you can decrease the recovery distance to 400 meters. If you have trouble completing the workout, increase the recovery interval.

Time/Distance	Pace	Elevation
10 Minutes	Warm Up	1%
1 Mile	5K pace	1%
1/2 Mile	Easy recovery pace	1%
1 Mile	5K pace	1%
1/2 Mile	Easy recovery pace	1%
1 Mile	5K pace	1%
1/2 Mile	Easy recovery pace	1%

5K Change of Pace

During a typical 5K race, you will not run at exactly the same speed the entire distance. You will more likely change your pace as you surge past other competitors and slow for a brief recovery. This workout simulates the change of pace that is necessary for top race performance.

After a warm up, run 1/2 mile at an easy pace, then speed up to 5K pace for 1/2 mile. Now slow down to 15 seconds per mile slower than 5K pace for 3/4 mile, then speed up to 10 seconds faster than 5K pace for 1/4 mile. Slow down to 15 seconds per mile slower than 5K pace for 1 mile, then finish with 1/10th of a mile at 20 seconds faster than 5K pace. Complete your workout with a 10 to 15 minutes cool down.

Time/Distance	Pace	Elevation
10 Minutes	Warm Up	1%
1/2 Mile	Easy pace	1%
1/2 Mile	5K pace	1%
3/4 Mile	15 seconds per mile slower than 5K pace	1%
1/4 Mile	10 seconds per mile faster than 5K pace	1%
1 Mile	15 seconds per mile slower than 5K pace	1%
1/10 Mile	20 seconds per mile faster than 5K pace	1%
10 Minutes	Cool Down	1%

Beginners Ladder

This is an entry level speed workout that is appropriate for beginners, but can also be used effectively by intermediate level runners.

After a warm up of 10 to 15 minutes, run 1 mile at an easy pace, then speed up to 10K pace for 1/2 mile. Then speed up again to 5K pace for 1/4 mile. There is no recovery between the different paces. Cool down with 10 to 15 minutes of easy running. Start with just one of these ladders. As your fitness level increases you can do two or even three of these short ladders.

Time/Distance	Pace	Elevation
10 Minutes	Warm Up	1%
1 Mile	Easy Pace	1%
1/2 Mile	10K Pace	1%
1/4 Mile	5K Pace	1%
5 Minutes	Cool Down	1%

Speed Ladder

This is a more advanced ladder workout that is designed for intermediate to advanced runners.

Warm up for 10 to 15 minutes. Then run 1 mile at 10 seconds per mile slower than your current 10K race pace. Now speed up to 10K pace for 3/4 mile. Then speed up to 5K pace for 1/2 mile. Finish the workout with 1/4 mile at 20 seconds per mile faster than 5K pace. There is no recovery between the various pace. Cool down with 10 to 15 minutes of easy running.

Time/Distance	Pace	Elevation
10 Minutes	Warm Up	1%
1 Mile	10 seconds per mile slower than 10K pace	1%
3/4 Mile	10K pace	1%
1/2 Mile	5K pace	1%
1/4 Mile	20 seconds per mile faster than 5K pace	1%
5 Minutes	Cool Down	1%

Reverse Ladder

This ladder workout will improve your speed and will also make increases in your lactate threshold and will train you to run at a quality pace when fatigued.

Warm up for 10 to 15 minutes. Start the workout with 1/4 mile at 10 seconds per mile faster than 5K pace. Then slow down to 5K pace for 1/2 mile. Now slow down to 10K pace for 3/4 mile. Finish with 1 mile at 10 seconds per mile slower than 10K pace. There is no recovery time between the different paces. Cool down with 10 to 15 minutes of easy running.

Time/Distance	Pace	Elevation
10 Minutes	Warm Up	1%
1/4 Mile	10 seconds per mile faster than 5K pace	1%
1/2 Mile	5K pace	1%
3/4 Mile	10K pace	1%
1 Mile	10 seconds per mile slower than 10K pace	1%
5 Minutes	Cool Down	1%

Beginners Pyramid

This is an entry level pyramid workout. Intermediate runners can also use this workout, especially early in their training season.

Warm up for 10 to 15 minutes. Begin your workout by running 3/4 mile at an easy pace. Speed up to 10K pace for 1/2 mile and then increase your speed to 5K pace for 1/4 mile or 400 meters. Now travel back down the pyramid by running 1/2 mile at 10K pace and finish with 3/4 mile at an easy pace. There is no recovery time between the different paces. Cool down with 10 to 15 minutes of easy running or walking.

Time/Distance	Pace	Elevation
10 Minutes	Warm Up	1%
3/4 Mile	Easy Pace	1%
1/2 Mile	10K Pace	1%
1/4 Mile	5K Pace	1%
1/2 Mile	10K Pace	1%
1/4 Mile	5K Pace	1%
10 Minutes	Cool Down	1%

Speed Pyramid

This is a challenging workout for advanced runners, that will test and improve your overall speed and your ability to maintain a quality pace when fatigued.

Warm up for 10 to 15 minutes. Then run 1 mile at your current marathon race pace. Speed up to 10K pace for 3/4 mile. Now increase your speed to 5K pace for 1/2 mile. Next speed up to a blistering 20 seconds per mile faster than 5K pace for 1/4 mile. Now run back down the pyramid, starting with 1/2 mile at 5K pace, followed by 3/4 mile at 10K pace and 1 mile at marathon pace. There is no recovery between the various paces. Cool down with 10 to 15 minutes of easy running or walking.

Time/Distance	Pace	Elevation
10 Minutes	Warm Up	1%
1 Mile	Marathon Pace	1%
3/4 Mile	10K Pace	1%
1/2 Mile	5K Pace	1%
1/4 Mile	20 seconds faster per mile than 5K pace	1%
1/2 Mile	5K Pace	1%
3/4 Mile	10K Pace	1%
1 Mile	Marathon Pace	1%
10 Minutes	Cool Down	1%

5 x 3 Minute Repeats

Here is another classic track workout that translates will to the treadmill. This workout is performed at a pace that approximately matches your vVO_2 max. The means your velocity at VO_2 max or the speed you are running when you reach the point at which your body is processing the most oxygen that it can. Training at this speed will improve your bodies ability to continue to produce energy when you are running at a highly intense pace and will also improve your running economy and your VO_2 max.

Warm up for 10 to 15 minutes. Then speed up to 15 or 20 seconds faster than your 5K pace. Run at this pace for 3 minutes. Then slow down to an easy pace for 2 minutes to recover. Repeat this sequence 5 times. Cool down for 10 minutes.

Time/Distance	Pace	Elevation
10 Minutes	Warm Up	1%
3 Minutes	3K Pace or 15 to 20 seconds faster than 5K pace	1%
2 Minutes	Easy Recovery Pace	1%
3 Minutes	3K Pace or 15 to 20 seconds faster than 5K pace	1%
2 Minutes	Easy Recovery Pace	1%
3 Minutes	3K Pace or 15 to 20 seconds faster than 5K pace	1%
2 Minutes	Easy Recovery Pace	1%
3 Minutes	3K Pace or 15 to 20 seconds faster than 5K pace	1%
2 Minutes	Easy Recovery Pace	1%
3 Minutes	3K Pace or 15 to 20 seconds faster than 5K pace	1%
10 Minutes	Cool Down	1%

Lactate Blasters

This is a highly effective but very tough treadmill speed workout that is really a lactate threshold or speed endurance workout in disguise. The best way to improve your speed endurance is by training your body to process accumulating lactate to produce energy more efficiently. What's the best way to do that? Flood your body with lactate and force your body to adapt itself in order to deal with it.

This speed workout does just that. The very fast repeats in this workout result in a rising level of lactic acid. Each repeat you do adds to the accumulation of lactic acid. Because of the constantly rising levels of lactic acid, this workout is sometimes called either lactate accumulators or lactate stackers.

After a 10 minute warm up run 6 to 12 one minute repeats at nearly full pace. You should not be at a sprint pace but very close to it. Your pace should be very close to your mile race pace or about 30 seconds per mile faster than your 5K pace. Recover between each 1 minute repeat with 2 minutes of easy jogging.

Time/Distance	Pace	Elevation
10 to 15 Minutes	Easy Warm Up Pace	1%
1 Minute	1 Mile Race Pace	1%
2 Minutes	Easy Recovery Pace	1%

Keep up that sequence of 1 minute at a very hard mile pace alternating with 2 minutes at an easy recovery pace. For your first attempt at this workout try for 6 repeats. As you become fitter and faster increase gradually increase your number of repeats.

Speed Compound Sets

Compound sets or supersets are runs of various distances or paces performed without recovery. A compound set is one the most effective ways to improve your fitness, speed and running performance. This is a speed based compound set.

After a 10 minute warm up begin this workout with 1.5 miles or 2400 meters at your current 10K pace. Then speed up to your current 5K pace for 1/2 mile or 800 meters. Take no recovery between the two segments of the set. Repeat that same compound set two more times for a total of 3 sets. Recover between each set with 2 minutes of passive rest.

Time/Distance	Pace	Elevation
10 Minutes	Easy Warm Up Pace	1%
1.5 miles or 2400 meters	Current 10K race pace	1%
.5 miles or 800 meters	Current 5K race pace	1%
2 Minutes	Rest	Rest

Repeat the above compound set two more times for a total of 3 complete compound sets. Remember that there is no recovery within the components of each set but you should take 2 minutes of passive rest for recovery between each of the three compound sets.

12

Hill Workouts

Hill training is hard. For that reason, some runners hate it and refuse to do it. I like hills. In fact, I love hills. I love hill training because it allows me to blow by the runners that don't do hill training. Yeah - it's hard, but the results are more than worth it.

Hill running is one the best and most efficient methods of training. Almost all top runners include hill workouts in their training program. Hill running improves your running specific strength, running economy, running mechanics, power, lactate threshold and aerobic conditioning. It also prepares you for the hills that you run into when you are racing.

There are three types of hill training that benefits runners.

- Hills that are included as part of a longer training run.
- Long hill repeats or one long consistent hill workout that is run at a strong, but maintainable pace.
- Short hill repeats run at a fast pace.

Hill runs are not easy workouts. They should be run at a pace that feels fairly hard, but not so hard that you cannot complete the entire workout at your planned pace. How hard you run the hills depends upon your specific level of fitness.

"Hills are speedwork in disguise"

-Frank Shorter

Hill workouts are perfect for the treadmill. Many runners are located in areas that have few hills. Even if you are located in a hilly area, you will probably have problems finding hills that will work perfectly for your planned workout. The treadmill removes this problem by providing hills of any length and at a wide range of inclines. It allows you to structure hill work that is very specific to your goals and your level of fitness. Most treadmills will adjust from zero to 12 percent incline, which will work well for almost all of your hill workouts.

The Foothills

This is an entry level hill workout. This training run is designed for more experienced beginning runners and intermediate runners that are new to hill training. You should be able to run 5 miles at an easy pace before you attempt this training run.

After a 10 minute warm up elevate the treadmill 1 percent and run at an easy pace for 1 mile, then raise the elevation to 2% and run for 3/4 mile. Raise the elevation to 3% and run for 1/2 mile then raise the elevation to 4% and run 1/2 mile. This is the "top of your hill". Now lower the elevation to 3% and run 1/2 mile; lower it to 2% and run 3/4 mile; and finally lower it to 1% and run 1 mile. Your total distance run in this workout is 5 miles. Keep both your pace and intensity at an easy level throughout this workout. You will need to decrease your pace as you increase elevation during this workout. If you attempt to maintain the same pace as the elevation increases, you will begin to work at a harder level than is appropriate for this workout. You should always feel that the intensity level is moderate to moderately hard.

Time/Distance	Pace	Elevation
10 Minutes	Warm Up	1%
1 Mile	Easy - Between 30 seconds and 1.5 minutes slower than marathon pace	1%
3/4 Mile	Easy - Between 30 seconds and 1.5 minutes slower than marathon pace	2%
1/2 Mile	Easy - Between 30 seconds and 1.5 minutes slower than marathon pace	3%
1/2 Mile	Easy - Between 30 seconds and 1.5 minutes slower than marathon pace	4%
1/2 Mile	Easy - Between 30 seconds and 1.5 minutes slower than marathon pace	3%
3/4 Mile	Easy - Between 30 seconds and 1.5 minutes slower than marathon pace	2%
1 Mile	Easy - Between 30 seconds and 1.5 minutes slower than marathon pace	1%

Hill Progression

This is a progressive hill workout that challenges you with increasing elevation levels, while maintaining a strong pace. The maximum elevation for this workout is 8 percent. This is a moderately steep grade, which makes this workout a good beginning to intermediate level hill run.

Warm up for 10 to 15 minutes. Increase the speed of the treadmill to about 20 seconds per mile slower than your 10K race pace. Run for 2 minutes with the treadmill elevated at 2 percent. Decrease the elevation to 1 percent and run for 2 more minutes. Now increase the elevation to 3 percent and run for 2 minutes. Decrease the elevation back to 1 percent and run for 2 minutes. Next increase the elevation to 4 percent and run for 2 more minutes, then decrease the elevation back to 1 percent for 2 minutes to recover. Keep up this pattern of increasing the elevation an additional percent for 2 minutes before decreasing back to 1 percent for a 2 minute recovery. Keep going until you reach 8 percent elevation.

Time	Pace	Elevation
10 Minutes	Warm Up	1%
2 Minutes	15 to 20 seconds slower than 10K pace	2%
2 Minutes	15 to 20 seconds slower than 10K pace	1%
2 Minutes	15 to 20 seconds slower than 10K pace	3%
2 Minutes	15 to 20 seconds slower than 10K pace	1%
2 Minutes	15 to 20 seconds slower than 10K pace	4%
2 Minutes	15 to 20 seconds slower than 10K pace	1%
2 Minutes	15 to 20 seconds slower than 10K pace	5%
2 Minutes	15 to 20 seconds slower than 10K pace	1%
2 Minutes	15 to 20 seconds slower than 10K pace	6%
2 Minutes	15 to 20 seconds slower than 10K pace	1%
2 Minutes	15 to 20 seconds slower than 10K pace	7%
2 Minutes	15 to 20 seconds slower than 10K pace	1%
2 Minutes	15 to 20 seconds slower than 10K pace	8%
5 Minutes	Easy pace cool down	1%

Rolling Hills

When running on a hilly training route or race course, you will encounter hills of various elevations and lengths. In order to be properly prepared for that type of terrain, you must practice and train using the same type of elevation changes. This workout is a difficult, but excellent long distance hill training run that uses hills of different grades.

Warm up for 10 to 15 minutes. Set the treadmill at about 30 seconds per mile slower than your current 10K pace. Set the elevation at 2 percent and run 1 mile. Now increase the grade to 5 percent and run another mile. Next decrease the grade to 2 percent and run for 1/2 mile. Now set the incline at 8 percent and run for 1/2 mile. Decrease the grade back to 2 percent and run another 1/2 mile. Now repeat the same pattern without recovery. Increase the incline to 5 percent and run for one mile. Next decrease the grade to 2 percent for 1/2 mile. Increase the incline to 8 percent for another 1/2 mile and then back to 2 percent for 1 mile. Cool down with 10 to 15 minutes of easy running.

Time/Distance	Pace	Elevation
10 Minutes	Easy - Warm Up	1%
1 Mile	30 seconds slower than 10K pace	2%
1 Mile	30 seconds slower than 10K pace	5%
1/2 Mile	30 seconds slower than 10K pace	2%
1/2 Mile	30 seconds slower than 10K pace	8%
1/2 Mile	30 seconds slower than 10K pace	2%
1 Mile	30 seconds slower than 10K pace	5%
1/2 Mile	30 seconds slower than 10K pace	2%
1/2 Mile	30 seconds slower than 10K pace	8%
1/2 Mile	30 seconds slower than 10K pace	2%
10 Minutes	Easy - Cool Down	1%

Hill Blasters

Most hill workouts are performed at easy to moderate paces. However, there are times during races that you will need to power strongly up a hill at race pace. If you do not practice that type of strong hill running, you will probably not be able to hold your pace during a race.

This is an intense hill workout that uses short runs up a steep grade. This training run is very good for building strength and power. This is a very difficult workout that is only appropriate for intermediate and advanced runners. Do not attempt this training run if you are not properly conditioned for highly intense physical activity.

Time/Distance	Pace	Elevation
10 Minute	Easy - Warm Up	1%
1/10th Mile	As fast as you can maintain for the entire workout.	10 - 12%
1 Minute	Easy recovery pace	1%
1/10th Mile	As fast as you can maintain for the entire workout	10 - 12%
1 Minute	Easy recovery pace	1%
1/10th Mile	As fast as you can maintain for the entire workout	10 - 12%
1 Minute	Easy recovery pace	1%
1/10th Mile	As fast as you can maintain for the entire workout	10 - 12%
1 Minute	Easy recovery pace	1%
1/10th Mile	As fast as you can maintain for the entire workout	10 - 12%
1 Minute	Easy recovery pace	1%

Keep up this pattern for your desired number of repetitions. You should not run these hill repeats until you are totally exhausted. For most runners it is better to be conservative and slightly under train rather than risk the potential injuries and other problems associated with over training.

Pike's Peak

This is a challenging hill pyramid workout of steadily increasing inclines followed by decreasing inclines. This workout will improve your running strength and your ability to handle steep hills while maintaining a quality pace. This is a difficult workout that should only be attempted if you are properly conditioned for high intensity training. If you become exhausted before running to the "top" of this hill, don't worry. Just stop climbing and begin descending down your hill at that point.

Time/Distance	Pace	Elevation
10 Minutes	Warm Up	1%
1/2 Mile	30 seconds slower than 10K pace	2%
1/2 Mile	30 seconds slower than 10K pace	3%
1/2 Mile	30 seconds slower than 10K pace	4%
1/2 Mile	30 seconds slower than 10K pace	5%
1/2 Mile	30 seconds slower than 10K pace	6%
1/4 Mile	30 seconds slower than 10K pace	7%
1/4 Mile	30 seconds slower than 10K pace	8%
1/4 Mile	30 seconds slower than 10K pace	7%
1/2 Mile	30 seconds slower than 10K pace	6%
1/2 Mile	30 seconds slower than 10K pace	5%
1/2 Mile	30 seconds slower than 10K pace	4%
1/2 Mile	30 seconds slower than 10K pace	3%
1/2 Mile	30 seconds slower than 10K pace	2%
10 Minutes	Cool Down	1%

Hill Fartlek

If there is such a thing as "fun" hill training, this is it. This is an unstructured training run. You decide when to throw in a hill and how steep to make the hill. You also decide what pace to run. Make this run different every time you perform it. When you do this run, do not plan your paces or elevations ahead of time. Just go with the flow and do whatever you feel like doing. The only rule is to change both pace and elevation frequently.

After a 10 to 15 minute warm up, run for 40 minutes. During your 40 minute run vary both the speed and the incline of the treadmill. Start out with easy running at a 1 percent grade. Then start to change both the elevation and the pace at your discretion. Do some short, steep hills at both an easy pace and at race pace. Do some longer hills, also at both an easy pace and at race pace. The idea of this workout is to get used to various paces and inclines. Do not run all of your steep hills at an easy pace. Make sure that you throw in some steep, fast hill work. This will make you familiar with any steep hill that you may run into during a race. This is a good entry level hill workout for beginners. If you are a beginning runner, limit the hill elevation to no more than 5 percent for the first few times. Once you have built up some strength in your tendons and muscle, you will be able to increase the elevation to higher levels. Many beginners have a tendency to hang on to the handles or railing of the treadmill when doing hill work. Try to avoid this. Hanging on to the treadmill defeats part of the training benefits of hill training. Have fun with this workout. The informal structure of this is something that you should enjoy and experiment with.

Time	Pace	Elevation
10 Minutes	Warm Up	1%
40 Minutes	Various paces between an easy pace and 5K pace	Various inclines between 1% and 12%

Beginner Hills

This is a entry level hill workout that is most appropriate for beginning runners. The maximum incline for this training run is 5%. The moderate elevation of the hills in this workout will allow a beginner to start to work on improving running strength and will also beef up those all important tendons and muscles that support the knees, hips and ankles. The prerequisite for attempting this workout is being able to run for at least 40 minutes without stopping and without having major discomfort.

Warm up for 10 to 15 minutes. Set the treadmill incline at 2% and run for 5 minutes. Increase the incline to 3% and run for another 5 minutes. Next, increase the grade to 4% and run for 5 minutes. Now decrease the incline back to 2% and run for 5 minutes. Increase the elevation to 5% and run for another 5 minutes. Decrease the incline back to 2% for 5 more minutes of running.

Time	Pace	Elevation
10 Minutes	Warm Up	1%
5 Minutes	Easy Pace	2%
5 Minutes	Easy Pace	3%
5 Minutes	Easy Pace	4%
5 Minutes	Easy Pace	2%
5 Minutes	Easy Pace	5%
5 Minutes	Cool Down	2%

The Hill Climb

This is a difficult workout that will challenge you both physically and mentally. If the shorter workouts are considered hill workouts, you may think of this one as a mountain workout. This workout will improve your strength in all race distances, but are especially efficient when training for longer 1/2 marathon or marathon races. Elite Kenyan runners are known for completing hill climbs as long as 20K.

Be sure to warm up thoroughly before this workout, because it will place a lot of stress on your muscles. After your warm up, set the treadmill at between 5% and 8% elevation. The elevation level that is appropriate for you will depend upon your specific level of experience and fitness. An intermediate runner should start with 5% and increase that as their fitness and strength level increases. A more experienced advanced runner could start with a higher elevation. Set the speed at approximately your marathon race pace. Run steadily at your chosen elevation level for between 2 and 10 miles. Your exact amount of mileage will also depend upon your experience and fitness level. Use your own judgment. This workout should be difficult, but be careful not to over estimate your fitness level. It is better to start with less mileage and see how your body reacts than to injure yourself with excessive mileage. An intermediate runner should start out with between 2 and 4 miles in this workout and advance as they gain strength. More experienced runners should start out at between 3 to 5 miles and increase accordingly.

Time/Distance	Pace	Elevation
10 Minutes	Warm Up	1%
2 to 10 miles	Marathon pace	5% to 8%
10 Minutes	Cool Down	1%

5K Hill Simulator

Most hill training is performed at slower than race pace. This improves your running strength, but does little to prepare you to run hills at race pace. This workout uses short hill repeats performed at race pace with recovery intervals on a level treadmill. This will train you to run hard and maintain a quality pace on hills encountered during a race.

Try to maintain 5K pace on each of the hard hill segments. The first few times you attempt this workout you may need to run those segments at 5K intensity or exertion level rather than actual 5K pace. 5K intensity is when you are running at what feels like 5K pace over flat terrain. Your actual pace may be slower but you are maintaining 5K intensity. As you become stronger you should be able to maintain your actual 5K pace during this workout.

Time/Distance	Pace	Elevation
10 Minutes	Warm Up	1%
1/2 Mile	Easy Pace	1%
1/4 Mile	5K Pace	3%
1/4 Mile	5K Pace	1%
1/4 Mile	Easy Pace	1%
1/4 Mile	5K Pace	5%
1/4 Mile	5K Pace	1%
1/4 Mile	Easy Pace	1%
1/4 Mile	5K Pace	8%
1/4 Mile	5K Pace	1%
1/4 Mile	Easy Pace	1%
1/4 Mile	5K Pace	3%
1/10 Mile	Easy Pace	1%
10 Minutes	Cool Down	1%

Tempo Hill Run

Hill running is tough enough when done as a separate workout. This treadmill workout makes it even tougher by combining a two mile tempo run with a hill training run. This is a challenging run but it also pays great benefits. This workout trains your body to run at a strong uphill pace when you're already somewhat fatigued. A perfect combination for race training, especially when your race includes hills. This is also a good workout for improving your lactate threshold as well as your overall fitness and strength.

First perform a 10 to 15 minute warm up, then run 2 miles at your tempo pace which is around 20 seconds per mile slower than your 10K race pace. This pace should feel moderate to moderately hard. After you finish your 2 mile tempo run, immediately increase your treadmill elevation to 3%. Run for 2 more miles at tempo pace increasing your treadmill elevation by 1% every quarter mile to a maximum of 10%. Then decrease your incline to 1% and cool down for 10 minutes.

Time/Distance	Pace	Elevation
10 Minutes	Easy Warm Up Pace	1%
2 Miles	Tempo Pace - about 20 seconds per mile slower than current 10K race pace. This pace should feel moderate to moderately hard.	1%
1/4 Mile	Same Pace	3%
1/4 Mile	Same Pace	4%
1/4 Mile	Same Pace	5%
1/4 Mile	Same Pace	6%
1/4 Mile	Same Pace	7%
1/4 Mile	Same Pace	8%
1/4 Mile	Same Pace	9%
1/4 Mile	Same Pace	10%
10 Minutes	Easy Cool Down Pace	1%
10 Minutes	Cool Down	1%

13

Long Runs

Long runs are one of the key workouts and are the cornerstone of long distance running. These long endurance runs are the workouts that, for many, bestow an identity to a distance runner. When the term "distance runner" comes up, it brings with it an image of a solitary athlete gliding smoothly along a rolling road or trail.

As all runners know, there is much more involved in training besides the long run. There is the interval training, the tempo work and the anaerobic threshold runs. We all like to run fast. We look forward to our speed work and lactate threshold runs where we can let it loose and fly. These fast paced workouts are critical in the development of speed and speed endurance. But, we cannot underestimate the importance of the weekly or biweekly long run.

The long runs improve our endurance. They train our body to run for long distances without stopping. They strengthen our muscles, joints and tendons so that we can avoid injury and support our faster paced runs. Long runs also train our minds. Long runs toughen us mentally so that we develop the ability to keep going even though our body is screaming at us to stop. All of these improvements are essential if we are to perform to the best of our abilities.

The training effects of long runs are cumulative. The payoff of these workouts build upon themselves week after week, month after month and year after year. You will get physically and mentally stronger. Your body will learn to store more and more energy providing glycogen, and your cardiovascular system will provide more and more oxygen to your muscles.

A long run should be included in your training program from once a week to once every three weeks, depending upon your goal, your experience level and where you are in your training cycle.

"The long run is what puts the tiger in the cat"

- Bill Squires

There are two different types of long runs:

• Easy Pace Long Runs - When most runners think of long runs this is the workout that they are doing. The pace is between 30 seconds slower than marathon pace to over one minute slower than marathon pace. The distance is anywhere from 10 miles up to 30 miles or 1 hour to over 4 hours. The distance and time depends upon your goal race and your fitness level.

• Goal Pace Long Run - This is a long run that is either partially or completely performed at your race goal pace. This long run can be used for any goal race distance, but is most commonly used for marathon training. If you are going to race a marathon, you must do some training at your goal race pace. The format can take several forms. It can be a long run in which a portion of it, usually the first part, is done at an easy pace and the last part is done at goal pace. This will train your body to run at goal pace for long distances while already fatigued. Goal pace can also be incorporated throughout a long run, much like a fartlek run. A fartlek run is a workout in which you change pace at your whim, without structure. In addition to multi pace runs, some medium distance long runs are done entirely at race pace.

Easy Marathon Run

This is a basic marathon training long run. The pace of this workout will vary from runner to runner, but should always be easy and "conversational" in nature. You should be running easy enough that you can carry on a conversation. For most runners it is somewhere around 1 minute per mile slower than marathon pace or 2 minutes per mile slower than 10K pace.

The distance of your first long run should be either 12 miles or the distance of your longest run in the past three weeks. The distance of each subsequent long run should be increased by one or two miles depending upon the amount of time until your goal race and your experience level. You should do a long run from one to three times per month. A beginning or intermediate level runner will probably perform better with only one or two per month, while a more experienced runner may be able to handle three per month. A first time marathoner should build up to a longest run of 18 to 22 miles. A more experienced runner may benefit from building up their long runs to the full race distance of 26 miles or even 27 or 28. These runs are performed at an easy pace, but should not be considered an easy run. The amount of time and distance involved make long runs a hard run and appropriate recovery time should be planned both before and after a long run.

Time/Distance	Pace	Elevation
5 Minutes	Warm Up	1%
12 to 26 Miles	About 1 minute per mile slower than marathon pace	1%
5 Minutes	Cool Down	1%

5K Long Run

Long runs are not used exclusively for marathon training. They are also used when training for shorter races from 2 miles to 1/2 marathons. Long runs improve your endurance and provide a base of fitness that you can build your entire training program around. If you are training for a 5K race, your long run should be approximately 10 miles in length. Since you are training to run at a pace that is much faster than your marathon pace, these shorter long runs are performed using both an easy pace and a goal race pace.

This is a long run used specifically to train for a 5K race. This workout will improve your aerobic conditioning, the ability of your body to deal with lactic acid and train your body to run at race pace when fatigued. This is a difficult workout that is geared toward the more experienced intermediate and advanced runners. Beginning runners should perform their 5K long runs entirely at an easy pace.

After a warm up, run three miles at an easy pace, then speed up to goal or current 5K pace for 1/2 mile. Slow back down to an easy pace for three more miles and then speed up again for 1/2 mile at race pace. Slow down to an easy pace for two miles and then speed up to 5K pace for one mile. Cool down with some easy running or walking.

Time/Distance	Pace	Elevation
5 Minutes	Warm Up	1%
3 Miles	Easy Pace	1%
1/2 Mile	5K Pace	1%
3 Miles	Easy Pace	1%
1/2 Mile	5K Pace	1%
2 Miles	Easy Pace	1%
1 Mile	5K Pace	1%
5 Minutes	Cool Down	1%

10K Long Run

Your 10K race pace is usually at or slightly faster than your lactate threshold. This is the pace at which your body starts to produce lactic acid faster than it can process it to produce energy. When lactate begins to accumulate, it leads to an acidic condition in your blood that inhibits your bodies ability to produce energy. This long run will help raise your lactate threshold which will allow you to run longer at a quality pace and will train you to run at race pace when fatigued.

This workout is specifically designed for 10K training, but because of its ability to improve your lactate threshold, it is also effective at 5K, half marathon and marathon training.

After a warm up, run 4 miles at an easy pace. Then speed up to 10K goal or current race pace for 1 mile. Slow back down to your easy pace for 4 more miles, then speed up again to your 10K pace for another mile. Now decrease your speed to an easy pace for 1.5 miles, then speed up to 10K pace for the final 1.5 miles. Cool down with some easy running.

This is a workout for intermediate to advanced runners. Beginning runners training for a 10K should do the entire run at an easy pace.

Time/Distance	Pace	Elevation
5 Minutes	Warm Up	1%
4 Miles	Easy Pace	1%
1 Mile	10K Pace	1%
4 Miles	Easy Pace	1%
1 Mile	10K Pace	1%
1.5 Miles	Easy Pace	1%
1.5 Miles	10K Pace	1%
5 Minutes	Cool Down	1%

Marathon Mimic

Long slow running is a valuable training tool. But it does not prepare you to run at your goal race pace. It is important to practice running at your goal marathon pace. Goal pace runs improve your running economy at race pace, mentally prepare you for the speed that you will be running and makes you more comfortable with your goal pace.

These workouts are performed by running at an easy pace for the first portion of your long run and then speeding up to goal pace for the last portion.

For your first goal pace workout, do the last 3 miles at goal marathon pace. For the ensuing runs, gradually increase the amount of goal pace running up to 12 to 15 miles. Intermediate runners should do no more than 12 miles at goal pace. More advanced runners could increase to as much as 15 miles. Beginning marathon runners should do no more than 6 miles at goal marathon pace.

This workout should be done anywhere from once per month to once every two weeks.

Time/Distance	Pace	Elevation
5 Minutes	Warm Up	1%
12 to 26 Miles	First Portion at an easy pace followed by the seconds portion at goal marathon pace.	1%
5 Minutes	Cool Down	1%

Marathon Mimic With a Kick

This workout is very similar to the Marathon Mimic. The difference is the addition of a kick to the end of the workout.

When doing this workout you will perform the first portion of your workout at an easy pace. Just as the Marathon Mimic you will then speed up to marathon pace for most of the second portion. During the last portion of this workout, you will speed up to 10K pace and finish the last 2/10th miles as fast as you can manage. This addition of faster that race pace running will help in two ways. It will simulate race conditions when you may need to pick up the pace at the end of the race and it will also help you prepare for hard running when you are already very fatigued.

There are many possible combinations of paces you can do. A good starting point would be running all but the last 4 miles of your long run at an easy pace, then speed up to marathon pace for 3 miles and finish with 1 mile at 10K pace followed by a sprint finish. As you progress through your training, you could gradually increase the distance of your marathon pace portion to 10 miles and the 10K kick to 3 miles. Do not do this workout more than once every 3 weeks.

Time/Distance	Pace	Elevation
5 Minutes	Warm Up	1%
12 to 26 Miles	First portion at an easy pace, second portion at marathon pace, finishing with a third portion at 10K pace and a sprint finish	1%
5 Minutes	Cool Down	1%

Marathon In The Middle

This is a marathon goal pace long run that includes a goal pace session in the middle of an easy paced long run. Placing the goal pace session in the middle of the run is a bit easier than doing the hard portion at the end of the run. That makes this training run more appropriate for the beginning and intermediate runner.

Do three miles at goal or current marathon pace, in the middle of your long run. For subsequent runs, increase the distance of the goal pace portion by one or two miles, up to a maximum of 12 miles. A beginning marathoner should limit the goal pace session to a maximum of 6 miles.

This workout should be done anywhere from one time per month to once every two weeks.

Time/Distance	Pace	Elevation
5 Minutes	Warm Up	1%
12 to 26 Miles	Easy pace with a some goal marathon pace running in the middle of the workout.	1%
5 Minutes	Cool Down	1%

Long Run Fartlek

This is a long run with a little spice. Run your scheduled long run distance at an easy pace. Every two or three miles, increase your speed to marathon goal pace for anywhere between 400 meters and 1 mile. You choose what speed and how often you do these goal pace surges. There is no strict structure to this run. Do not use the same distance for all of your surges. Do some long surges and some short. This run should be fun, but also serves a valuable service. It prepares you for the different paces that you will be running during your race.

Time/Distance	Pace	Elevation
5 Minutes	Warm Up	1%
12 to 26 Miles	Easy pace with surges at marathon goal pace of between 800 meters and 1 mile.	1%
5 Minutes	Cool Down	1%

Heartbreak Hill

This is a great workout for training for the Boston Marathon or any marathon that has hills at the middle or end of the course. This run takes its name from the famous Heartbreak Hill that is located between miles 20 and 21 on the Boston Marathon course. This training run incorporates several hill sessions into a standard long run. The hill intervals will build strength, running economy and prepare you to meet the challenge of a hilly marathon course.

The 1 mile segment at zero elevation is intended to simulate the downhill portion of the Boston course. If your treadmill will decline use a minus 2% to 3% decline for this segment.

This training run can also be shortened to use earlier in your training cycle or if you are not conditioned for a 21 mile run. Simply insert the hilly portions of the workout approximately 1/2 to 3/4's of the way through your run. For example, if your run is 12 miles in length, insert the hills at anywhere from 6 to 9 miles into your workout.

Time/Distance	Pace	Elevation
5 Minutes	Warm Up	1%
15 Miles	Easy Pace	1%
1/2 Mile	Easy Pace	3%
1 Mile	Easy Pace	1%
1/2 Mile	Easy Pace	4%
1 Mile	Easy Pace	1%
1/2 Mile	Easy Pace	6%
1 Mile	Easy Pace	1%
1/2 Mile	Easy Pace	8%
1 Mile	Easy Pace	0%
5 Minutes	Cool Down	1%

10K Marathon Repeats

This is a goal pace marathon run that uses 10K intervals performed at goal pace.

After a warm up, run a 10K at your goal marathon race pace. Recover after the 10K run with easy running or walking for 5 to 10 minutes. Repeat this for a total of 2 to 4 repeats, depending upon your experience and fitness level. This is a difficult workout and should be progressively built up in order to avoid overtraining problems and potential injury.

This training run is also a progressive run. The first time you do this workout, do two repeats. As your fitness level improves increase the number of repeats.

Time/Distance	Pace	Elevation
5 Minutes	Warm Up	1%
10K	Goal marathon pace	1%
5 Minutes	Easy recovery	1%
10K	Goal marathon pace	1%
5 Minutes	Easy recovery	1%
10K	Goal marathon pace	1%
5 Minutes	Easy Recovery	1%
10K	Goal marathon pace	1%
5 Minutes	Cool Down	1%

5K Marathon Repeats

This training run is similar to the 10K marathon repeats, except it uses 5K repeats instead of 10K repeats. This shorter distance makes it a more appropriate workout for beginners. It can also be used very effectively by intermediate and advanced runners.

After a warm up, run 5 kilometers at your goal marathon pace. Recover with 5 minutes of easy running or walking. Repeat this 4 to 8 times depending upon your fitness and experience level.

This is a strenuous workout that should be performed no more than once every three weeks.

Time/Distance	Pace	Elevation
5 Minutes	Warm Up	1%
5K	Marathon goal pace	1%
5 Minutes	Easy pace	1%
5K	Marathon goal pace	1%
5 Minutes	Easy pace	1%
5K	Marathon goal pace	1%
5 Minutes	Easy pace	1%
5K	Marathon goal pace	1%
5 Minutes	Easy pace	1%
5K	Marathon goal pace	1%
5 Minutes	Easy pace	1%
5K	Marathon goal pace	1%
5 Minutes	Easy pace	1%
5K	Marathon goal pace	1%
5 Minutes	Easy pace	1%
5K	Marathon goal pace	1%
5 Minutes	Cool Down	1%

Commercial Cruncher

Who says television commercials are a waste of time? I think they provide a valuable service to distance runners. Have I lost my mind? Maybe - but I don't think so. How about using those commercials to increase your fitness and running performance?

Here is a workout that makes good use of television commercials. Do do this workout you will need a television in front of your treadmill. I like to watch TV when I am running on my treadmill. I usually feel a little guilty when I am lounging on the couch watching a movie or show. I feel like I should be doing something more productive. When I watch television while doing my daily treadmill workout it's like guilt free TV time. How do you use the commercials to improve your fitness? Easy - just plan a workout that is the same length as your favorite TV show or movie. Run at your normal easy endurance pace for the length of your workout. Here is the fun part. Every time a commercial comes on speed up to your marathon pace. Keep up that marathon pace for the duration of the commercial and then slow back down to easy endurance pace for the show.

Time/Distance	Pace	Elevation
The same time frame as the show or movie you are watching	Run at your easy endurance pace during the show. Increase your speed to marathon pace for the duration of each commercial.	1%

The Big Trail

This one is for all you mountain trail runners out there. It can be tough to get your trail running fix in the winter when the trails are snow packed, icy and treacherous. Here is a 14 mile treadmill hill climb that, while it can't replace running on a mountain trail, it will at least give you some of the strength and fitness benefits of a long hill climb.

Time/Distance	Pace	Elevation
1 Mile	Easy Endurance Pace	2%
1 Mile	Easy Endurance Pace	3%
1 Mile	Easy Endurance Pace	5%
1 Mile	Easy Endurance Pace	3%
.5 Miles	Easy Endurance Pace	8%
1 Mile	Easy Endurance Pace	5%
.5 Miles	Easy Endurance Pace	10%
1 Mile	Easy Endurance Pace	5%
.5 Miles	Easy Endurance Pace	12%
1 Mile	Easy Endurance Pace	5%
.5 Miles	Easy Endurance Pace	10%
1 Mile	Easy Endurance Pace	5%
.5 Miles	Easy Endurance Pace	8%
1 Mile	Easy Endurance Pace	3%
1 Mile	Easy Endurance Pace	5%
1 Mile	Easy Endurance Pace	3%
.5 Miles	Easy Endurance Pace	2%

Index

R

Running on the Treadmill

S

Speed Endurance Workouts

Speed Workouts

T

Training Methods

Treadmill Advantages

Treadmill Disadvantages

Treadmill Features

LaVergne, TN USA
23 February 2011
217646LV00002B/323/P